I0095350

The Nigerian Deception…

Authored By
Lee Feigum

Prologue

This story was inspired by my personal experiences in Nigeria many years ago. Enough time has passed that the individuals involved are no longer among us, posing no threat to me or my family.

While the narrative draws from real events, it has been heavily fictionalized. The names, places, and circumstances have been altered, and any resemblance to actual persons, living or dead, is purely coincidental.

This is a story of ambition, deception, and survival — a reminder that sometimes the most dangerous deals are the ones that never make the headlines.

Dedication

To those who warned me—your voices echoed long after I stepped onto the plane. To the shadows behind this story—gone now, but not forgotten. And to those who still know the truth behind the fiction... thank you for keeping your silence.

Author Bio

Lee Feigum is a career real estate broker and entrepreneur with a deep love for international travel and true- story thrillers. After a real-life brush with an elaborate scam in Nigeria, Lee transformed that experience into his debut geopolitical novel, The Nigerian Deception.

When he's not writing, Lee enjoys RV,ing , historical research, and crafting stories that blend business acumen with pulse-pounding suspense. He lives in the Pacific Northwest and is currently working on the second Carter Weston novel, The Biafra Cipher

.

Copyright © 2025 by Lee Feigum

All rights reserved. No part of this publication may be reproduced, distributed, or transmitted in any form or by any means, including photocopying, recording, or other electronic or mechanical methods without the prior written permission of the author except in the case of brief quotations embodied in reviews and certain other non-commercial uses permitted by copyright law.

Published by
Brookscraft Publishing
A Division of Brooks Craft LLC
Info@brookscraftpublishing.com
www.brookscraftpublishing.com

Author's Contact

To book the author as a speaker at your next event or to order bulk copies of this book, please, use the email below:

Lfeigum587@gmail.com

Table Of Content

Prologue ii

Dedication iii

Author Bio...iv

Table Of Content...vi

Chapter 1: The Letter...1

Chapter 2: Due Diligence 4

Chapter 3: The Proposal 7

Chapter 4: Stepping into the Unknown 10

Chapter 5: "The Visa Visit" 12

Chapter 6: The Island Introduction 17

Chapter 7: Shadows beneath the Surface.........................23

Chapter 8: The Meeting...31

Chapter 9: The First Test...37

Chapter 10: The Package 42

Chapter 11: The Delivery...46

Chapter 12: A Warning...50

Chapter 13: Nowhere to Run 59

Chapter 14: A Dangerous Proposition...............................62

Chapter 15: A Desperate Gamble 65

Chapter 16: The Blue Orchid 68

Chapter 17: Nowhere to Hide 73

Chapter 18: The Noose Tightens 76

Chapter 19: A Race Against Time 81

Chapter 20: A Dangerous Proposition...............................83

Chapter 21: The Final Offer 86

Chapter 22: A Desperate Gamble 89

Chapter 23: The Escape Clause................................92

Chapter 24: A Shadow That Follows......................96

Chapter 25: The Weight of a Name.........................99

Chapter 26: The Shadow on the Plane............... 102

Chapter 27: Nowhere to Run 106

Chapter 28: An Exit at 35,000 Feet..................... 110

Chapter 29: The Lisbon Gamble 114

Chapter 30: Running for His Life.......................... 118

Chapter 31: A Narrow Escape 122

Chapter 32: – The Call for Help 125

Chapter 33: Meeting Tariq.................................... 128

Chapter 34: The Favor 132

Chapter 35: The Heist 136

Chapter 36: A Narrow Escape 140

Chapter 37: Nowhere to Hide 143

Chapter 38: The Escape Route.............................. 146

Chapter 39: Into the Unknown 149

Chapter 40: The Turning Tide.............................. 152

Chapter 41: Adrift in the Dark 157

Chapter 42: The Escape... 160

Chapter 43: A Safe Harbor?.................................. 162

Chapter 44: A Fragile Refuge................................ 165

Chapter 45: The Man in the Shadows 168

Chapter 46: Calculated Moves 171

Chapter 47: Crossing the Threshold 174

Chapter 48: Closing In 177

Chapter 49: The Pursuit 181

Chapter 50: Safe Harbor 185

Chapter 51: The Villa 189

Chapter 52: A New Path 193

Chapter 53: Unfinished Business 200

Chapter 54: Into the Horizon 204

Epilogue 206

Chapter 1: The Letter

It started out as a day like any other at ICC Corp. (International Communications), a company I founded that was steadily growing, securing small but meaningful contracts in the telecommunications sector. We were a respected name in the industry, known for reliability and expertise. I was always on the lookout for the next big opportunity—something that could push us to the next level.

So, when a letter arrived from Lagos, Nigeria, printed on crisp, official-looking stationery, I took notice.

The sender introduced himself as Solomon Adewale, an electrical engineer who had come across our company's logo in a prestigious industry publication. His tone was professional, his English impeccable, and his proposition—if even half-true— was staggering.

According to Adewale, before a recent military coup had upended the Nigerian government, $18,000,000 had been allocated to modernize the country's outdated telecommunications infrastructure. The project had been approved at the highest levels, and the funds had already been placed in a government-controlled account, ready for disbursement. But then the regime changed, chaos erupted, and the project was abandoned. The money, however, remained untouched—lost in the bureaucratic maze of Nigeria's financial system.

Adewale claimed he had inside access to these funds, along with a trusted associate—a senior banker—who could facilitate their release. Their problem was simple: they needed a legitimate foreign company to serve as the recipient. That's where ICC Corp. came in. If I agreed to help "repatriate" the money through offshore accounts, my company would be awarded a fabricated contract, complete with official purchase orders and invoices. Everything would appear above board. In return, I would receive a staggering $5,000,000 as a token of their appreciation.

It sounded too good to be true.

A deal like this could change everything. If it was legitimate, ICC Corp. could use the funds to move from a respected mid-level player to a global force in telecommunications. But a nagging thought lingered in the back of my mind. Deals like this—too perfect, too effortless—rarely turned out the way one hoped. There were whispers of fraud schemes in international business, stories of entrepreneurs who had chased easy money only to lose everything.

Still, what if this was real?

I leaned back in my chair, staring at the letter. This warranted further investigation. At the very least, I needed to know more.

Chapter 2: Due Diligence

Carter had built ICC Corp. on a foundation of calculated risks, but he wasn't reckless. Before engaging with Solomon Adewale, he needed to verify as much as possible. In 1990, international telecommunications weren't what they are today—there was no instant Googling of names, no quick background checks. Business dealings in distant countries often relied on word of mouth, faxes, and costly international phone calls that had to be scheduled in advance.

I placed the letter on my desk and exhaled slowly. The offer was staggering—almost too perfect—but experience had taught me that in business, if something seemed too good to be true, it usually was.

Still, I wasn't about to dismiss it outright. Not yet.

Before I even considered responding, I needed to verify Solomon Adewale's claims. If there was any truth to the supposed telecommunications fund, I'd find it. And if this was an elaborate scam, I'd know soon enough.

I started with the basics. A quick scan of my industry contacts yielded no prior knowledge of Adewale. No one had worked with him, heard of him, or even recognized his name. That wasn't necessarily a red flag—Nigeria's telecom sector was in flux, and new players were constantly emerging—but it did little to reassure me.

Next, I reached out to a banking associate who specialized in international finance. Keeping my inquiry vague, I asked about the legitimacy of large government contracts in Nigeria and whether such funds could exist in limbo after a coup. His response was cautious but revealing.

"Theoretically possible," he admitted, "but highly unlikely. Government accounts don't just sit unclaimed, especially in volatile regions. Someone, somewhere, would have seized control. "

That gave me pause.

I dug deeper, researching Nigeria's recent political upheaval. The country had seen a series of coups over the years, and its financial system was notoriously opaque. Corruption was rampant, and money often disappeared into bureaucratic black holes. If there was any country where $18,000,000 could go unnoticed, Nigeria was it.

But the real test came when I checked Adewale's references. In his letter, he had mentioned a partnership with a senior banker, Ibrahim Hassan—someone allegedly powerful enough to release the funds. Lacking local contacts, I sent a discreet inquiry through our company's' banker, who was a member of an international banker's association, to verify the man's existence. The response came back quickly.

"Hassan is a highly placed banker," the reply read. "However, proceed with extreme caution

Chapter 3: The Proposal

Carter leaned back in his chair after the call, staring at the ceiling. Solomon had been confident, smooth even, but that wasn't unusual in business. Carter had spent years negotiating international deals, encountering plenty of smooth talkers along the way. Yet, there was something different about Solomon—an assurance that went beyond typical business bravado. The real question was whether this was an opportunity or a trap.

The next day, a fax arrived on ICC Corp. letterhead—though not from his office. It was from Solomon, who had taken the liberty of drafting an official-looking purchase order for telecommunications equipment. The order was for $18 million in infrastructure, with ICC listed as the primary vendor. The Nigerian government, he claimed, would approve the transfer upon receipt of invoices.

Carter reviewed the document carefully. ICC Corp. had successfully handled telecommunications contracts in multiple countries before, so he knew what to look for. The formatting and official seals were in place, but something about it felt off. It had the right formatting and official seals, but something about it felt off. He picked up the phone and dialed the number Solomon had given him.

"Ah, Carter, "Solomon answered on the second ring. "I trust you received the documents. "

"I did," Carter said. "It all looks very. ... Efficient. But I have a few concerns. "

Solomon chuckled. "Concerns are natural in business, my friend. Tell me, what troubles you? "

"For one, I'd like to know exactly who is authorizing this. Government contracts usually require more than a signature from a banker and an engineer. "

"Ah, but this is why we act swiftly, " Solomon replied smoothly "The officials who were involved before the coup have disappeared, and those in power now prefer discretion. It is why we need a reliable partner like you. "

Carter frowned. That answer wasn't particularly reassuring. But before he could press further, Solomon added, "If it helps, I can arrange a meeting. Come to Lagos. See for yourself. "

Carter hesitated. A trip to Nigeria wasn't exactly a casual decision. But if there was even a sliver of truth to this, the reward could be immense.

"I'll think about it," Carter said finally.

"Do not think too long," Solomon warned. "Opportunities like this do not wait forever."

Carter hung up and stared at the fax once more. This was getting real—fast.

Chapter 4: Stepping into the Unknown

The decision to go to Nigeria wasn't one Carter made lightly. He had lingering doubts about Solomon's assurances and the legitimacy of the deal. Every instinct told him to proceed with caution, yet the potential payoff was too enticing to ignore. He spent days weighing the risks and potential rewards, consulting with trusted colleagues, and researching as much as he could about doing business in Lagos. The more he learned, the more he realized just how unpredictable the situation could be.

Before committing to anything, Carter placed a discreet call to an old acquaintance from his college days — now a mid-level analyst at the U. S. State Department. The two hadn't spoken in years, but Carter trusted his judgment and knew he'd offer an honest assessment. The voice on the other end was cautious. "Be careful, Carter. The political climate is unstable, corruption is rampant, and foreign businessmen often find themselves entangled in bureaucratic nightmares — or worse. You won't have the same protections there as you do here. If something goes wrong, it'll be difficult to get you out. " Despite the warnings, Carter knew that big opportunities required bold action.

The weeks leading up to my departure were a blur of preparations. I had to move carefully, balancing my curiosity with the need for caution.

First, I needed a visa.

Chapter 5: "The Visa Visit"

Obtaining a visa on short notice required an in-person visit to the Nigerian Embassy at 3519 International Court NW in Washington, D. C. Carter arrived early, dressed in a conservative suit, hoping to project the kind of professionalism that would make the process smoother. But as soon as he stepped through the doors, he knew it wouldn't be simple.

The waiting area was sparse but dignified—marble tile floors, framed photographs of Nigerian landscapes and leaders, and a slight chill in the air that didn't quite match the warmth of the staff's expressions. A uniformed attendant took his documents and gestured for him to wait.

It wasn't long before a tall, impeccably dressed man emerged from a side door and called Carter's name.

"I am Mr. Olayemi, the ambassador's attaché," he said, shaking Carter's hand with a practiced firmness. "Please, come with me."

The interview room was small, with high ceilings and a single flag of Nigeria standing proudly behind a desk. Carter sat across from the attaché, who began reviewing his application with a slow, deliberate air.

"Mr. Weston, your request is unusual. What is the nature of your travel to Nigeria? "

"I'm a telecommunications consultant," Carter replied evenly. "I've been invited to discuss a potential infrastructure project."

Olayemi raised an eyebrow. "By whom?"

Carter paused. "A Nigerian national named Solomon Adewale."

The attaché's fingers stopped drumming the tabletop. He leaned back slightly, eyeing Carter with fresh scrutiny. "And what is the purpose of this... arrangement?"

"It's preliminary," Carter said carefully. "If the deal is real, I'm there to perform due diligence. Nothing more. "

Olayemi tapped his pen on the table, then asked, "Do you understand the risks involved in doing business in Nigeria at this time?"

"I've been briefed," Carter said. "I'm aware of the political volatility and... let's say, bureaucratic complexity."

The attaché gave a knowing smile. "A diplomatic way of putting it." Then his tone shifted, his gaze sharpening. "Mr. Carter, be honest with me. Are you being lured into a scam? "

Carter didn't flinch. "If I am, I'll find out soon enough. But I need to see it for myself. "

Olayemi studied him for a long moment, then stood. "Very well. We don't normally expedite visas unless there is government sponsorship. But we also recognize that certain opportunities don't come twice. "

He stepped to a filing cabinet and returned with a stamped document. "You'll have your visa by this afternoon. Good luck, Mr. Weston. "

Carter stood to shake his hand. "Thank you."

Olayemi held onto his grip just a second longer than expected. "Just remember… in Lagos, luck is never free."

With the expedited visa secured from the Nigerian Embassy in Washington, D. C. , and vaccinations complete, Carter stepped back out into the sharp spring air with more questions than answers. The attaché's parting warning— "Even in diplomacy, trust is rarely free"—echoed in his ears as he flagged down a cab. He was closer now, but nowhere near ready to commit. If he was going to dive into this deal, he needed more than just a visa and blind faith. His next move had to be strategic. Before boarding a plane to Lagos, Carter made arrangements for a quick detour—one that would lay the groundwork for everything that followed. He needed an offshore account. Not just a placeholder, but a well-structured financial instrument that could shield him if things went south. And there was no better place for that than George Town, Cayman Islands. He knew the optics mattered. Showing Solomon and his associates that he was financially prepared sent a message: I'm serious— but I'm not naive. If this transaction was real, they'd have a destination for the funds. If it wasn't, the account gave him leverage—an escape hatch he could control from offshore. He finalized his plans, ensuring that his affairs were in order before booking his flight.

With the expedited visa from the Nigerian Embassy in Washington, D. C., and all required vaccinations, he was ready for George Town.

Chapter 6: The Island Introduction

The heat in George Town was thicker than he remembered — a sticky, sun-soaked embrace that wrapped around Carter the moment he stepped off the jet. It wasn't unpleasant. In fact, it reminded him of his sailing days in the Caribbean, of warm evenings on deck with a glass of rum and nowhere particular to be. But this trip wasn't for nostalgia. It was for insurance.

The visit to the Cayman Islands had been impulsive, at least on paper. But Carter never trusted large transfers or foreign accounts he hadn't personally vetted. That was just good business. When you were dealing with men like Solomon Adewale — men who claimed to have access to millions trapped in limbo — you needed to have an escape hatch.

Barclays Bank Cayman was housed in a sleek glass-and-stone building at 25 Main Street, just a block from the waterfront. It was modern, understated, and guarded by the kind of security that didn't wear uniforms but watched everything.

Carter stepped into the air-conditioned lobby and gave his name. Moments later, a woman appeared at the far end of the marble floor and glided toward him with the confident stride of someone who knew her way around power.

"Mr. Weston," she said with a smile. "Welcome to George Town. I'm Marielle Thomas, Senior Relationship Manager. We're honored by your visit. "

She extended a hand. Her grip was firm, her eyes assessing — sharp and dark, with the kind of depth that made Carter instinctively more cautious.

Marielle was striking. Mid-thirties, a native islander by her lilt and complexion, with sleek black hair tied into a low knot and a designer watch that told him she wasn't just successful — she was meticulous.

"Appreciate you making the time," Carter said. "I like to know who I'm trusting with my money."

"And we like to know our clients value discretion," she replied, motioning him toward a private elevator.

Her office overlooked the harbor — a floor-to-ceiling view of sailboats gliding across the turquoise sea. A decanter of something expensive gleamed on a sideboard.

"Tell me," She said as they sat, "what's the nature of the account you wish to open?"

"Offshore trust," Carter replied. "Needs to be nimble. But protected. Not much paper trail."

Marielle didn't blink. She nodded slowly, typing a note into her tablet.

"Of course. We specialize in confidential structuring. And you'll find our fiduciary services are second to none. " She paused, then added with a hint of amusement, "But I assume you've already done your homework."

Carter smiled. "I wouldn't be here if I hadn't."

After an hour of reviewing forms, encryption options, and transfer protocols, she leaned back in her chair and smiled in a way that softened her otherwise professional demeanor.

"I think we've covered the essentials," she said. "Now comes the fun part."

Carter raised an eyebrow.

She stood and walked to the sideboard. "There's a tradition we have for new high-value clients," she said. "A drink — on the bank's tab. Welcome to the island."

"You're not the first client from West Africa we've assisted recently," Marielle said with a flicker of a smile. "There's been. ... A surge in activity tied to telecom and infrastructure funds. Oddly synchronized. "

Carter raised an eyebrow. "Coincidence?"

She didn't answer directly—just poured the drinks.

She poured two glasses of single malt and handed him one.

"To clean starts and complicated clients," she toasted, clinking her glass against his.

Later that evening, they sat on a shaded terrace at a harbor-front lounge. Talk drifted from business to travel, to the slow erosion of trust in a world that ran on secrets and silence. The sea lapped gently against the dock just beyond them, and the glow of the lanterns gave the whole scene a golden softness.

At one point, Marielle leaned in, swirling her drink, her voice lowering with curiosity.

"You don't seem like the kind of man who trusts easily," she said.

"I don't," Carter replied, not missing the way her eyes held his just a second longer than expected. "Comes with the territory."

She smiled at that — not coy, but thoughtful. "I'd say that's smart. But it must get lonely, always looking for the exit. "

Carter glanced at the ocean, then back at her. "Sometimes. But occasionally, you meet someone who makes you forget to look. "

It was quiet after that. Comfortable. Charged.

She raised her glass.

"To unexpected company, then."

"And complicated clients," he echoed with a smirk.

They didn't touch hands. They didn't make promises. But when Carter stood to leave, Marielle reached out briefly and straightened the collar of his shirt.

"Just… be careful, Mr. Weston," she said, her tone soft. "Even the safest harbor can hide dangerous currents."

Carter's smile faded, just slightly. It wasn't what she said. It was how she said it.

By the end of the evening, the account was open, the protocols were in place, and Carter had an encrypted access key tucked into the lining of his passport wallet. But as he walked back to his hotel in the humid night air, her words lingered.

Even the safest harbor…

Chapter 7: Shadows beneath the Surface

The next morning, Carter awoke to the sound of gulls and the distant rumble of a ferry pulling into port. His suite at the Caribbean Club offered the best view money could buy — a wide, uninterrupted horizon framed by sheer white drapes and a balcony that smelled faintly of jasmine and sea salt.

Still, he hadn't slept well.

He sat at the edge of the bed, watching the sun lift over the horizon like a slow burn. The encrypted access key from Barclays was on the dresser beside his passport and a burner phone he'd picked up in New York. It was all there — clean, tight, secure.

But something still nagged at him.

Marielle's parting words from the night before lingered.

"Even the safest harbor can hide dangerous currents."

He dressed quickly, pulled on a linen shirt and khakis, and made his way down to the lobby. The air was already thick with heat and the scent of diesel from the ferries leaving port.

"Mr. Weston," the concierge called out. "Someone left this for you."

The man handed him a cream-colored envelope. No name. No return address. Inside, there was only a single business card.

White. Minimalist. Raised lettering.

S. Owusu

International Investments – Advisory Division

On the back, a handwritten note:

It's not too late to walk away. Some tides can't be outrun.

Carter stared at the card for a long moment. He turned it over once, then again. Clean stock. No watermark. He slipped it into his wallet without a word.

"Did you see who left it?"

"Courier," the concierge replied. "Local outfit. No name. "

Outside, the harbor was coming alive. Fishermen prepping lines. Crews untying charter boats. A pair of kids zipped past on electric scooters, laughing.

Everything looked normal.

But something had shifted.

The name Owusu stirred something in the back of his mind. Briefings. A note scribbled in a margin during a closed-door meeting. A man with ties to African finance… and intelligence.

He flagged a cab and gave the driver his destination. At the airport, Carter moved through security with his usual ease, checked a decoy briefcase containing nothing of importance, and boarded the British Airways flight bound for Heathrow.

As the plane lifted into the sky and the island faded beneath him, he gazed out the window, jaw set.

The harbor was calm. The sky was clear. But a storm was coming.

And Carter Weston wasn't planning to wait it out.

His flight route took him from George Town to London, where he transferred to British Airways for the final leg to Lagos. During the layover, he double-checked his documents, mentally reviewing his cover story and rehearsing possible explanations for his visit. He replayed Solomon's words in his head, trying to gauge the risks and assess whether he was walking into an opportunity or a trap. Each mile brought him closer to an uncertain reality—one that would test his instincts like never before. He leaned back in the business-class seat, the low hum of the engines lulling his thoughts into a drift. Lagos was still hours away, but his mind was already racing ahead, cataloging contingencies and exit strategies.

And yet... part of him still hesitated.

He had been here before—not to Nigeria, but to this place of ambition teetering on risk.

Years ago, in the early days of ICC Corp., Carter had flown into Caracas with a briefcase full of contracts and confidence. It was his first major international venture—a joint infrastructure project

25

with supposed government backing. The meetings had been smooth, the assurances louder than the alarms in his gut. They'd toasted the deal with rum on a balcony overlooking the city lights.

Three weeks later, the bank transfer failed.

His contact—trusted, or so he thought—had vanished. The contracts had been signed, sealed, and meaningless. When Carter returned to Venezuela to confront someone—anyone—he found nothing but locked doors and closed ranks. A shift in political winds, they said. The government had changed, the ministries had been "restructured," and the deal was now void. No refunds. No apologies.

He'd nearly lost the company then.

Carter shifted in his seat, glancing down at the folder by his side. Inside were the purchase orders Solomon had promised, the structure of the deal that could make—or unmake—him.

He wasn't that wide-eyed operator anymore. Not by a long shot. He'd rebuilt after Caracas. He'd learned to watch the margins, the tone of a voice, and the flicker in a man's eyes when he talked about money.

Still, something about Solomon's charm and the speed of the deal felt uncomfortably familiar.

And that old feeling was back—the one that said he was stepping onto a chessboard, not a balance sheet.

He rubbed a hand over his face, letting the hum of the jet pull his thoughts further back—before

Caracas, before contracts and currency exchange rates, to a time when his world was measured in knots and latitude.

There was a season—two years, maybe three— when Carter lived almost entirely on his sailboat, drifting between island ports like a man with nothing to prove. He'd launched from the Keys and island-hopped down to Grenada, taking odd consulting gigs along the way to fund his journey. He fished in the mornings, negotiated dock fees with a smile, and spent his evenings barefoot on the deck, watching the constellations shift overhead like a slow-turning compass.

He remembered a night off the coast of Bequia. No cell signal. No responsibilities. Just a gentle breeze off the beam and the sound of waves against the hull. He had anchored near a British couple who invited him aboard for rum and stories. They asked what he did for a living, and he told them, "Nothing permanent."

For once, it felt true.

The sea had given him something no balance sheet could offer: silence, clarity—and the reminder that not every course needed a map.

He missed that life sometimes. Not enough to go back, maybe. But enough to know what peace looked like when it was real.

Now, bound for Nigeria, wrapped in layers of logistics, diplomacy, and deception, he wondered if he could ever reclaim that kind of freedom again.

Maybe not.

Or maybe this deal, however dangerous, was a means of returning to it.

As the plane descended toward Murtala Muhammed International Airport, he felt the weight of uncertainty settle in his chest. He was stepping into the unknown, and there was no turning back now. Warnings from colleagues and the State Department echoed in his mind—cautionary tales of business deals gone wrong, of foreign investors who found themselves ensnared in corruption and bureaucracy. Yet, despite the red flags, Carter had made his choice. The thrill of the unknown and the promise of fortune outweighed the fear. Now, all he could do was trust his instincts and move forward.

Arriving near midnight to sweltering heat and suffocating humidity, Carter made his way through customs while enduring interrogation like questions about his presence in Nigeria from unsmiling personnel in military uniforms. Not what Carter expected to encounter in an international airport.

Passport stamped and carryon searched, Carter scanned the terminal for a mode of transportation to his hotel. Seeing Carters puzzled look, a uniformed man with an official looking badge asked, where to?

The Hilton, Carter replied, and was met with a smile and assurances that for $20 he could make that happen. Carter eagerly handed over the fee and was led briskly to the terminal exit where they were abruptly halted by two uniformed military personnel who demanded to know where Carter was headed. Satisfied with the response Carter was allowed to leave the terminal wondering if what the guards really wanted was a cut of the $20.

Once outside, Carter was assaulted with dozens of cries of "Car for Hire". No shuttle service so Carter caught a ride to the Hilton in a battered 1970 Volvo with no air conditioning for twenty U. S. dollars---clearly, a popular number among the locals. Carters' driver, Kofi, was a young college student who shared with Carter, his plans for the future, which included a visit to Disneyland someday. Arriving at the Hilton, Kofi retrieved Carters carryon and offered Carter the following advice. Be careful who you trust!

At the hotel, he was met with another jarring reality. Carter received his room key and as he approached the elevator, he found it guarded by armed military. The guard, noticing Carter's startled expression, smirked and said, "Surely, you wouldn't wish for some unscrupulous fellow to creep in under the cover of night and slit your throat, would you?"

Carter swallowed hard, realizing just how far he was from the world he knew. He was in the lion's den now, and there was no turning back.

The rest of the night slipped away, sleep refusing to come as memories of the past days and the uncertainty of what lay ahead crowded my mind.

Chapter 8: The Meeting

The morning sun barely cut through the thick haze of Lagos as I stepped outside the Hilton. The heat was already oppressive, wrapping around me like a wet blanket. A black Mercedes idled at the curb; its windows tinted dark enough to obscure whoever sat inside. As I approached, the rear passenger door opened.

"Mr. Weston, please, get in," a voice urged from within.

I hesitated, glancing around. Kofi's warning from the night before still echoed in my mind. "Be careful who you trust". But I had come too far to back out now. I slid into the seat, the door shutting firmly behind me.

Solomon Adewale sat across from me, dressed in a tailored suit that seemed at odds with the chaotic city outside. He was younger than I had expected, perhaps in his late forties, with sharp eyes that studied me as if calculating every move before making it.

"Mr. Weston, it is a pleasure to finally meet you, "he said, offering a firm handshake. "I trust your accommodations are satisfactory? "

"They'll do, "I said, keeping my tone neutral, friends call me Carter. "You mentioned a complication. "

Solomon nodded, his expression darkening. "Yes. The process of moving the funds has encountered. ... Resistance. Certain officials require additional assurances to facilitate the transaction."

I arched a brow. "How much are we talking?"

He sighed, glancing out the window as we pulled onto a congested road. "Fifty thousand dollars. In cash. It will ensure the necessary approvals. "

I let that sink in. This wasn't just about an offshore account anymore. This was about cold, hard cash changing hands in a country where trust was a dangerous commodity.

Solomon smiled, but there was something in his eyes that told me he already knew I'd come prepared. "I assure you, Carter, it is merely a formality. Once the officials are satisfied, the funds will be released without delay. You will be paid handsomely for your efforts. "

"That's a hefty sum to produce on short notice," I said, keeping my tone measured. But I had already taken precautions—Chase, my company's bank, had been alerted in advance that I might need to withdraw a significant amount from their Lagos branch. "

Before they could retrieve the funds from Chase Bank, Solomon insisted on one more stop—a meeting with Ibrahim Hassan, a senior official at the Central Bank of Nigeria. The car eased its way through the morning traffic to Tinubu Square, the financial heart of Lagos. The stately stone facade of the bank loomed over the street like a fortress.

Inside, the contrast was stark—air-conditioned silence, polished floors, and guards who scanned every visitor with hawk-like intensity. Solomon led the way through a series of internal corridors until they were ushered into a private conference room.

Ibrahim Hassan stood to greet them; his expression unreadable. Tall, with a commanding presence and immaculate suit, he extended a hand to Carter.

"I've heard a great deal about your firm," Hassan said, motioning them to sit. "Let's discuss the release protocol."

What followed was a calculated, precise exchange. Hassan explained that while the funds were earmarked, they would be transferred in tranches—each triggered by the presentation of corresponding invoices and government-approved documentation. The Central Bank, he stressed, would only act on official government authorization.

"The Cayman Islands account will receive only what is documented, Mr. Weston," Hassan concluded. "No more, no less. You understand? "

Carter nodded, suppressing the knot in his gut. Everything about the setup was technically above board—but that didn't mean it wasn't dangerous.

Solomon stood, smoothing his jacket. "We appreciate your clarity, Mr. Hassan."

As they exited the bank, Solomon clapped Carter on the back. "A formality, my friend. Now, let's visit our friends at Chase. "

As they return to the car, Solomon tossed a worn leather folder onto the seat between them, loosening his tie with a casual flick. Carter caught a glimpse as the folder cracked open slightly—papers stamped in heavy red ink and a logo he didn't recognize: a falcon perched on a shield; the Latin motto too blurred to read.

Before Carter could study it further, Solomon snapped the folder shut with a smooth motion.

"Old contracts from other ventures," Solomon said lightly, as if reading Carter's mind. "In my business, you learn to diversify."

Carter nodded, but the image of that insignia lingered like a stubborn shadow. Diversification was one thing. This smelled like something else entirely.

"The Chase Bank on 11 Michael Olawale-Cole Drive was bustling with activity, but the sharply dressed manager, Mr. Adebanjo, efficiently produced the requested funds, placing them in Carter's well-worn briefcase, while Solomon waited in the Mercedes, the air conditioner humming softly."

Carter thanked Mr. Adebanjo with a firm handshake and made his way back to the waiting Mercedes, the briefcase secure in his grip. Sliding into the passenger seat, he gave Solomon a nod. Without a word, Solomon's driver eased the car back into the flow of traffic.

The car slowed, weaving through a narrow street lined with market stalls and street vendors. I noticed two men on a motorcycle trailing us, their faces partially obscured by scarves. Solomon followed my gaze and chuckled softly.

"Do not worry," he said. "They are just keeping an eye on things. A precaution. "

A precaution.

I wasn't sure whether that was meant to reassure me or unsettle me further. Either way, I was now in deeper than I had ever planned.

Chapter 9: The First Test

The Mercedes pulled to a stop in front of an unmarked building, its weathered facade blending into the dense sprawl of Lagos. Solomon gestured for me to stay put as he stepped out, speaking briefly with a man in a beige suit who had been waiting by the entrance. I couldn't hear the conversation, but their body language suggested a mixture of tension and familiarity.

Carter couldn't help but notice how effortlessly Solomon secured appointments with ministers and directors—people who normally guarded their time like gold. It wasn't just charm; it was as if invisible hands were clearing the path ahead of him.

Already, Solomon had lined up multiple meetings for the coming days with senior government officials—contacts Carter would have struggled to even approach back home. And this was only the beginning.

As they pulled up to the first of these appointments, Carter felt the surreal weight of it all. Less than twenty-four hours in Lagos, and he was already being swept into the upper echelons of Nigerian bureaucracy as if it were all preordained.

It nagged at me, but I chalked it up to local influence and money well spent. I had bigger things to worry about.

After a moment, Solomon motioned for me to follow. "Come, Carter. We must meet with the facilitator. "

I climbed out of the car, adjusting to the sweltering heat once again. The two men on the motorcycle from earlier had stopped a short distance away, their presence a silent reminder that I was being watched. Whether it was for my protection or otherwise, I couldn't be sure.

As Carter reached for the door, Solomon caught his arm. "Be careful what you say—and who hears it, "he said quietly. "There are eyes you'll never see, watching. "

I nodded, thinking he meant the usual political paranoia. I didn't realize he meant something far worse.

Inside, the air was thick with the scent of cigars and old paper. The room was sparsely furnished, save for a large wooden desk and a few chairs. Behind the desk sat an older man with graying hair, his suit slightly rumpled but his demcanor authoritative. His sharp eyes locked onto me the moment I stepped through the door.

"Mr. Weston," he said, his accent thick but his English precise. "I am Mr. Okoye. You come here to do business? "I nodded, shaking his outstretched hand. "That's right. Solomon said there was an issue. "

Okoye chuckled, shooting a glance at Solomon. "An issue? No, no — just a matter of trust. Here in Nigeria, trust isn't given freely. It's earned — and usually at a price, "he said, pouring a generous measure of vintage Scotch into our glasses.

I kept my expression neutral, waiting for him to continue. He leaned forward, steepling his fingers.

"Before we proceed, we need assurance that you are fully committed to this arrangement. A small demonstration of faith. "

Solomon handed him the briefcase containing the recently withdrawn funds, which Okoye opened, flipping through its contents before nodding. He then turned his attention back to me.

"Your money is safe, Mr. Weston. But to move forward, we need to see how you handle pressure. A simple delivery—nothing more. A package needs to be taken to a government official. You will do this personally. "

I frowned. "That wasn't part of the deal."

Okoye smiled, but it didn't reach his eyes. "Consider it an opportunity to show your seriousness. If you cannot complete this task, then perhaps you are not the right man for this venture."

I glanced at Solomon, who gave a barely perceptible nod. Solomon leaned back in his chair, swirling the amber liquid in his glass.

"You know, Carter," Solomon said casually, "in this part of the world, it's not the buyer who wins — it's the man who owns the pipeline."

I raised an eyebrow, puzzled, and he caught the reaction immediately.

Solomon chuckled, but there was a glint in his eye — sharp, calculating — that made me wonder if he was only half-joking.

I exhaled slowly. I had come this far.

"Alright," I said. "Where's the package?"

Chapter 10: The Package

Okoye slid a small, leather-bound case across the desk toward me. It was no larger than a cigar box, but its weight suggested something of value inside. I hesitated before picking it up, my pulse quickening as I felt the cool, firm edges beneath my fingertips.

"What's inside?" I asked, keeping my tone even.

Okoye smiled, but his eyes remained unreadable. "That is not your concern. Your task is simply to deliver it to the Ministry of Trade and Investment. There, you will ask for a man named Chief Ekwueme. He will be expecting you. "

I exhaled through my nose, nodding slowly. "And if I refuse?"

Solomon shifted beside me, his body tense. "That would be. ... Unwise. "

The air in the room seemed to grow heavier. I understood the unspoken threat. This was no longer a business arrangement; it was a test, and failure was not an option.

Okoye leaned back in his chair. "You leave now. A car will take you. "

I took the package and stood. The weight of it in my hands felt disproportionate to its size, as though I carried something far more dangerous than I realized. Solomon gestured for me to follow, and we stepped back into the blinding Lagos sun.

The same black Mercedes was waiting at the curb, the driver holding the door open. I slid inside, placing the case carefully on my lap as Solomon followed.

"You must not open it," he said quietly as the car pulled away. "Do you understand?"

I met his gaze, searching for any hint of deception. "I understand."

The drive was silent, the tension thick. As we weaved through the congested streets, my mind raced through the possibilities. Was I carrying a bribe? Classified documents? Something worse?

As the Mercedes wound through the choking Lagos traffic, Carter let his eyes drift across the chaos outside—vendors shouting over heaps of electronics, taxis jostling for position, the scent of diesel thick in the air.

Solomon's phone vibrated against the center console. He picked it up without hesitation, pressing it to his ear with an air of practiced calm.

"Proceed with the second phase. No delays, "Solomon said quietly, his voice dropping low. "Tell them to expedite the approvals. "

Carter kept his gaze trained on a passing danfo, pretending not to listen. Second phase? Approvals? He filed the odd phrasing away, a pebble of unease settling in his gut. When Solomon ended the call, he offered Carter a genial smile. "Routine logistics. Nothing to worry about. "

But Carter wasn't so sure.

Twenty minutes later, the car eased to a stop in front of a government building, its concrete exterior weathered from years of neglect. A uniformed guard at the entrance barely glanced at me as I stepped out, package in hand.

"I'll be waiting here," Solomon said. "Go. Find Chief Ekwueme. "

I adjusted my tie and swallowed the unease creeping up my spine.

One way or another, I was about to find out just how deep I had gotten myself into.

Chapter 11: The Delivery

The interior of the Ministry of Trade and Investment was a stark contrast to the chaotic streets outside. The air was cool, humming with the soft buzz of fluorescent lighting. A handful of bureaucrats moved about, their faces betraying varying degrees of disinterest and exhaustion.

I approached the reception desk, gripping the leather-bound case firmly. The woman behind the counter, dressed in a crisp blue uniform, barely glanced up.

"I'm here to see Chief Ekwueme," I said, keeping my voice steady.

Her fingers drummed lazily against the desk as she eyed me. "Do you have an appointment?"

"He's expecting me. Tell him it's about the package. "

She pursed her lips but picked up the phone, muttering in a local dialect before setting the receiver down. "Third floor. Office at the end of the hall. "

I nodded in thanks and made my way to the elevator. Each floor we passed only added to the weight in my chest. Was I walking into a simple exchange, or was this something far more dangerous?

The doors slid open to a dimly lit hallway. At the far end, a wooden door stood slightly ajar. I moved toward it, forcing my steps to remain measured. I knocked twice and stepped inside.

Chief Ekwueme was an imposing figure, his broad shoulders filling the space behind his desk. He looked up from a pile of papers, his expression unreadable.

"Mr. Weston," he said, motioning for me to sit. "I see Solomon trusts you."

I placed the case on the desk. "I was told to deliver this to you."

Ekwueme studied me for a long moment before undoing the clasps and lifting the lid. He peered inside, his face betraying nothing, then carefully closed it again.

"You're either very brave or very foolish," he said, leaning back. "Do you know what you've just transported?"

I shook my head. "I was told not to ask."

He let out a low chuckle. "Smart man. Perhaps too smart."

The air in the room grew thick with unspoken tension. Whatever was in that case, it was worth more than money. And I had just placed myself squarely in the middle of something far beyond what I had signed up for.

Ekwueme folded his hands. "Tell Solomon the delivery is complete. You may go."

I stood, my legs slightly unsteady, and turned for the door. As I stepped into the hallway, I exhaled sharply, trying to shake the feeling that I had just crossed a line I could never uncross.

I had done what was asked. But I wasn't sure if I was any closer to getting out of this alive.

Chapter 12: A Warning

As I stepped out of the Ministry of Trade and Investment, the Lagos heat hit me like a wall. The black Mercedes was still waiting at the curb, Solomon leaning casually against it, his arms crossed. He watched me approach, his face unreadable.

"Did he accept it?" Solomon asked, his voice level.

I nodded. "No issues. He just told me to tell you the delivery is complete. "

Solomon exhaled, glancing around before motioning for me to get in the car. As soon as the door shut, the driver pulled away from the curb.

"You did well," Solomon said after a moment. "Most foreigners would have asked too many questions. That can be dangerous. "

I adjusted my tie, still trying to shake the tension from the meeting. "What was in the case?"

Solomon turned to me, his expression suddenly colder. "I told you not to ask."

A silence stretched between us as the car wove through the congested streets. I glanced out the window, my mind racing. I had delivered the package, but I had a sinking feeling that this was far from over.

We drove in silence for nearly twenty minutes. Solomon pulled the car into a gated lot behind a modest office building, cutting the engine with a satisfied grunt.

"Quick stop," he said, flashing a rare, easy smile. "Just need to grab a document. Then we celebrate properly. "

The office was sparse and cool, with the faint buzz of a faulty light overhead. A single desk sat at the center of the room, and a battered file cabinet hunched against the far wall.

"Make yourself comfortable," Solomon said, disappearing into an inner room. The door clicked shut behind him.

Carter waited—at first.

His eyes drifted to the desk, where a leather folder sat half-open. Papers spilled out, neat but hurried.

Curiosity gnawed at him. Instinct pushed harder.

Quickly, Carter stepped forward. Inside the folder, the top page wasn't an invoice or a contract— it was a detailed map, marked with infrastructure hubs, telecom routes, shipping manifests. Company names he didn't recognize were linked together with red arrows.

And at the bottom of the page, a single chilling word: Leverage. Another page beneath it listed foreign company names—some crossed out, others circled. One was flagged in red:

"Westgate Minerals - Johannesburg - Compromised."

Carter quickly snapped a photo, his stomach sinking. This wasn't about telecom. It was a pattern.

Without thinking, Carter pulled out his phone and snapped photos of everything he could.

He had just tucked the folder back into place when Solomon's voice called from the back.

"Ready, Carter?"

Carter straightened, forcing a casual smile as Solomon reappeared, keys jangling in his hand.

"Let's eat," Solomon said, taking him by the arm, "You've earned it."

Carter followed him out, the weight of what he had just seen pressing heavier with each step.

The restaurant Solomon chose was tucked into a side street just off the Marina, one of those polished little gems meant for men who dealt in quiet power.

Soft jazz curled through the air like smoke. Low voices murmured over heavy plates and expensive wine.

Solomon was in high spirits.

He ordered without even glancing at the menu, waving off the waiter with the practiced ease of a man who knew he belonged.

Carter sat across from him, outwardly relaxed.

Inside, though, his mind spun like a storm.

Leverage.

Infrastructure maps.

Shell corporations.

It wasn't what Solomon said — it was what he didn't say.

No mention of the project timeline anymore. No excitement about the transfer of funds. No questions about Carter's progress.

Instead, Solomon talked about art. About travel. About the future.

"The future belongs to those who seize it," Solomon said, raising his glass. His eyes gleamed with a quiet satisfaction that set Carter's teeth on edge.

Carter forced a smile and clinked glasses.

He told himself he was overthinking. That he was reading shadows into candlelight.

But deep down, a cold certainty settled into his gut:

Solomon's phone buzzed sharply on the table.

He glanced at it once, face unreadable, then silenced the call without answering.

I caught a glimpse of the name flashing on the screen — something foreign, not from our recent contacts. "Problems?" I asked, keeping my tone light. "Nothing worth mentioning," Solomon said, sliding the phone into his pocket. "Focus on the bigger picture, Carter. Always the bigger picture. "

Soloman spoke more to himself than to Carter. "Sometimes," he muttered, eyes distant, "the real victory is hidden the wreckage of the first plan."

"You know, Carter," Solomon said, swirling the wine in his glass, "sometimes we work for things much larger than ourselves. Bigger forces, bigger futures. "He left it at that, a cryptic smile flickering across his face. "Let's just say," he continued, swirling his wine, "I'm not the only one interested in seeing this deal succeed. And some of those watching... don't ask for second chances." Carter forced a chuckle, but the chill crawling up his spine didn't go away.

I let it slide, assuming he was just trying to sound impressive. At the time, I still thought I understood the game we were playing.

Following dinner, Solomon swirled his wine and leaned in. "You should leave Lagos soon."

I raised an eyebrow. "Why?"

He took a sip of wine before responding. "Because now, you're involved. And trust me, Mr. Carter, involvement has consequences. "

Carter leaned back, studying him. "I came here for a business deal. You're making it sound like something else. "

"Careful, Carter. In this part of the world, hesitation gets a man killed. "

Solomon wasn't preparing to close the deal.

He was preparing to disappear.

And Carter?

He was just another loose end waiting to be tied off.

The night air hit Carter like a slap when he stepped out of the restaurant — heavy with salt, diesel, and something harder to name.

Solomon clapped him on the back, a little too hard, and laughed at some private joke Carter wasn't sure he understood.

"Rest up, my friend," Solomon said, his grin flashing under the streetlights. "Big things ahead."

Then he was gone — swallowed by the Mercedes idling at the curb, leaving Carter standing alone on the cracked sidewalk.

For a long moment, Carter didn't move.

The city buzzed around him — neon flickering, distant horns blaring — but it all felt muted, like he was underwater.

Trust isn't given freely. It's earned — and usually at a price.

Okoye's voice echoed in his mind.

Kofi's warnings.

The hidden maps.

The word Leverage, printed in cold black ink.

Carter shoved his hands deep into his jacket pockets and started walking, keeping his head down, blending into the crowd.

One more job, Solomon had said.

One more hand to shake, one more formality to sign.

But Carter knew now — deep in his bones — that whatever Solomon had planned; he wouldn't need Carter much longer.

And men like Solomon didn't leave loose ends.

He needed me to stir the waters — to kick up enough chaos that no one would notice what he was really stealing.

And now, Solomon had everything he wanted.

The infrastructure.

The leverage.

The future.

And Carter?

Just another loose end to be cleaned up.

Outside, the humid night pressed against him.

Carter slipped into the shadows, heart pounding — not with fear now, but with something colder:

Resolve.

Chapter 13: Nowhere to Run

The warning sat heavy in my mind long after I left Solomon at the hotel lounge. The message was clear—I needed to get out of Lagos, and fast. But something told me that leaving wouldn't be as simple as booking a flight home.

Back in my hotel room, I locked the door and reached for the phone. I dialed the international operator, requesting a call to my business partner in the States. The line crackled before a familiar voice came through.

"Carter? You alright? "

"Not sure yet, "I admitted. "I need you to check on something for me. The account at Barclays in the Caymans—has there been any activity? "

There was a pause before he responded. "Yeah. A deposit came through this morning. A little over fifty thousand. "

I felt my stomach tighten. This wasn't supposed to happen yet. "From where?"

"Unclear. It's been routed through a couple of places, but it traces back to an offshore entity in—get this—Abuja. "

Abuja. The political heart of Nigeria. My pulse quickened. Someone had moved money into my account, and it sure as hell wasn't me.

A knock at the door made me jump. My heart pounded as I crept toward the peephole. A man in a dark suit stood outside, his expression unreadable.

"Mr. Weston," he called. "We need to talk."

I took a step back, my mind racing. Who was he? Government? A rival player in this twisted game?

Another knock—harder this time. "We know you're in there. Open up. "

Every instinct screamed at me to run, but I was boxed in. Lagos wasn't a city you could disappear in easily, not as a foreigner. My options were running out, and fast.

Taking a deep breath, I reached for the door handle. Whatever was coming, there was no avoiding it now.

I opened the door.

Chapter 14: A Dangerous Proposition

The man in the dark suit stepped inside without waiting for an invitation. Two others followed, their expressions cold and unreadable. The door clicked shut behind them, sealing me in.

"Mr. Weston," the first man said, his voice smooth but firm. "My name is Inspector Adeyemi. I work with the Economic and Financial Crimes Commission. "

My pulse pounded in my ears. EFCC. Nigeria's financial crime unit. This was bad—very bad.

"We have reason to believe you are involved in an illegal financial operation," Adeyemi continued, motioning to a folder in his hand. He flipped it open, revealing copies of documents I recognized—wire transfer records, emails, even a copy of Solomon's letter. "Your presence here raises many questions."

I forced myself to remain calm. "I came here for a business deal. If there's been any wrongdoing, I'm as much a victim as anyone. "

Adeyemi tilted his head, studying me. "That may be. Or you may be playing a dangerous game, knowingly or not. Either way, you are in a precarious situation. "

The second man, silent until now, stepped forward. "There is a way to resolve this quietly. You help us, we help you. "

I narrowed my eyes. "Help you how?"

"We need information on Solomon Adewale. His dealings have attracted interest at high levels. If you cooperate, we can ensure you leave Nigeria unscathed. If not..." He let the sentence hang in the air.

A cold knot formed in my stomach. I was being pulled in deeper, whether I liked it or not. Betray Solomon, or risk getting swallowed by a system I barely understood.

Adeyemi leaned in. "Think carefully, Mr. Weston. You don't have much time. "

The room felt smaller, the walls closing in. I had come here chasing a business opportunity, and now I was trapped in a web of corruption and power plays.

I needed a way out. And fast.

Chapter 15: A Desperate Gamble

The room felt like it was closing in on me. Inspector Adeyemi and his men were waiting for an answer, their expressions unreadable, yet filled with an unspoken threat. If I refused to cooperate, I had no doubt that my departure from Nigeria would be anything but smooth—if I was allowed to leave at all.

"I need time to think," I said carefully, trying to buy myself some breathing room.

Adeyemi smiled, but there was no warmth in it. "Of course. But not too much time. Lagos is not a city for hesitation. We will be in touch. "

With that, he snapped the folder shut and gestured to his men. One of them leaned in before leaving, his voice barely above a whisper. "Watch yourself, Mr. Weston."

As soon as they were gone, I locked the door and exhaled sharply. My mind was racing. Solomon had warned me about getting involved. Now I was in the middle of something I barely understood, with powerful people on all sides. I needed to find a way out before it was too late.

I reached for the phone and dialed Solomon's number. It rang three times before he answered, his voice low. "Carter. You're still in Lagos? "

"I just had a visit from the EFCC," I said, keeping my voice steady. "They want me to turn on you."

There was a long pause. Then, in a measured tone, Solomon said, "We need to meet. Now. Somewhere discreet. "

I hesitated. "Where?"

"There's a club in Victoria Island. The Blue Orchid. Be there in an hour. "

The line went dead.

I grabbed my jacket and took a deep breath. This was a dangerous game, and I was running out of moves.

One way or another, tonight would determine my fate in Nigeria.

Chapter 16: The Blue Orchid

The drive to Victoria Island was tense. The taxi wove through the chaotic streets of Lagos, past crumbling buildings and neon-lit billboards advertising everything from mobile services to bottled water. I kept glancing at the rearview mirror, half-expecting to see a tail. Whether it was the EFCC or someone worse, I wasn't sure.

The Blue Orchid was tucked into a quieter part of Victoria Island, its unassuming entrance manned by a pair of burly doormen who gave me an once-over before stepping aside. Inside, the dim lighting and smoky air gave the club a shadowy, conspiratorial feel. A jazz band played in the corner, their melancholic notes barely cutting through the low murmur of hushed conversations.

I spotted Solomon at a secluded booth near the back, his eyes scanning the room before settling on me. He gestured for me to sit.

"You were followed?" he asked, his voice barely above a whisper.

"Not that I saw," I said, though I wasn't entirely sure.

I expected anger when I laid out the problems—the tightening security, the nervousness from the Nigerian contacts. Instead, I got something else.

Solomon simply leaned back in his chair, fingers steepled under his chin. "Setbacks are just

ripples in the current, "he said coolly. "Stay the course.
"

It chilled me more than if he'd lost his temper.

As Carter and Solomon finalize logistics for the fund transfer in the back of the restaurant, papers spread out between coffee cups and empty plates, Carter tapped his pen against a draft of the transfer agreement. "So once the funds are repatriated, we can finalize the movement to the Cayman account."

For the briefest moment, Solomon's easy smile faltered. His eyes darkened.

"Repatriated," he echoed, almost as if tasting something sour.

He leaned forward, lowering his voice. "Money is just a vehicle, Carter. A means to an end. Real power lies in who controls the movement—not who holds the deed. "

He straightened, smile back in place, but the air between them had shifted.

Carter forced a nod, even as a cold thread of uncertainty snaked through him.

He wasn't dealing with a desperate businessman. He was dealing with a strategist. A player on a much bigger board.

Solomon exhaled sharply and leaned forward. "Carter, you need to leave Lagos. Tonight. "

"And how exactly am I supposed to do that? The EFCC has my name flagged, and I doubt they'll just wave me through security. "

Solomon slid a folded piece of paper across the table. "There's a man. A pilot. He flies out of a private airstrip near Badagry. He owes me a favor. If you can get to him, he can get you out. "

I unfolded the paper, scanning the handwritten directions. "And what about you?"

Solomon smiled grimly. "My path is different. You were never meant to get this deep, Carter. Now I have to clean up this mess before it gets worse. "

Something in his tone sent a chill through me. "You're not coming, are you?"

He shook his head. "I have unfinished business. But you—you may have a chance to walk away. Take it. "

I wanted to argue, to tell him there had to be another way. But deep down, I knew he was right. I had stumbled into something far bigger than I had realized, and every second I stayed, my chances of survival dwindled.

I stood up, slipping the paper into my pocket. "Solomon…"

He held up a hand. "Go. Before it's too late. "

I nodded once, then turned and walked out, barely glancing at the black Mercedes parked at the curb, the weight of the night pressing heavy on my

shoulders. I had one chance to escape, and I wasn't
going to waste it.

Chapter 17: Nowhere to Hide

Carter knew he had to move fast. The realization hit him the moment he stepped out of The Blue Orchid—this wasn't just a bad deal; it was a deadly trap. Solomon's demeanor had shifted. The once-slick businessman now radiated quiet menace, and the nervous glances told him everything he needed to know.

The streets of Lagos were alive with movement even at this late hour—vendors pushing carts, groups of men huddled in dim alleyways, the occasional roar of a passing motorbike. He ducked into the shadows, scanning his surroundings before pulling out the slip of paper in his pocket. It was a number—someone Solomon had given him as a "trusted contact." Carter didn't trust it one bit.

Instead, he reached for his own lifeline: a contact at the U. S. consulate. A man named Harrington, who had warned him before about getting too deep into Nigerian business. He found a payphone, shielding himself from prying eyes, and dialed.

The phone rang once. Twice. A third time.

"Harrington," a gruff voice answered.

"It's Carter. I'm in trouble. "

A pause. Then, "Where are you?"

"The Hilton. But I need to get out. Now. "

Another pause. Then, a low curse. "Stay put. I'll see what I can do. "

Carter hung up, but he knew better than to stay in one place. He slipped through a back alley, keeping to the darkest corners. He had one shot at this—if he made a mistake, he wouldn't get another chance.

His plan was simple: get a driver, get to the airport, and get the hell out.

But nothing in Lagos was ever simple.

As he hailed a cab, a black Mercedes pulled onto the street behind him. The same one that had been parked outside The Blue Orchid.

Carter's gut twisted. He wasn't out of this yet.

Chapter 18: The Noose Tightens

Carter sat rigid in the backseat of the rusting Peugeot as it weaved through Lagos' chaotic night traffic. The driver, a gaunt man with sharp eyes, hadn't spoken a word since Carter slipped him a stack of naira and uttered a single command:

"Airport. Fast. "

His heart pounded against his ribs. Every shadow felt like a threat, every passing vehicle a potential tail. Solomon's warning echoed in his mind:

You don't just walk away from this.

They barreled through a crowded roundabout, the Peugeot's suspension groaning as it bounced over a pothole. Carter wiped a hand across his forehead. Sweat, or nerves—probably both. Then he saw them.

Just as they turned onto the airport access road, headlights flared in the mirror—a black Mercedes with tinted windows, moving aggressively through the lane behind them.

"Faster," Carter barked.

The driver didn't answer. He simply gritted his teeth and slammed his foot down. The old Peugeot coughed and surged forward, threading recklessly through swerving danfos and swarming Okada's.

Behind them, the Mercedes was relentless. It clipped a taxi, skidded around a bus stop, and kept coming.

"That car's not here to wave goodbye," Carter muttered.

Then came the flash of metal. A rear window of the Mercedes slid down.

Gun.

"Down!" Carter shouted as a round punched through the back window, spraying glass across the seats. A scream tore from a pedestrian as the Peugeot fishtailed, barely missing a fruit cart that exploded into the street.

People screamed and scattered. Horns blared.

"Cut right! Alley—now! " Carter yelled, spotting a narrow gap between a shuttered pharmacy and a paint-chipped wall.

The driver didn't hesitate this time. Tires squealed as the car dove into the alley, scraping one side on a rusted metal gate. The Peugeot bounced through potholes and garbage piles, its shocks howling in protest.

The Mercedes overshot the turn and screeched to a halt, reverse lights blinking as it tried to follow.

Carter looked behind them—no clear line of sight. Good. But not good enough.

The alley spit them out onto a service road bordering the airport's perimeter. The flashing control tower lights rose in the distance like a beacon. But the road was open—too open.

"Can we make it to the cargo entrance?" Carter asked.

The driver nodded grimly, turning hard onto a gravel service lane.

Then—headlights again. Same car.

"Persistent bastard," Carter hissed.

They roared past a chain-link fence, nearly hitting a uniformed guard on a motorbike. Another shot cracked—this one sparking off the roof just inches above Carter's head.

"No more bullets, okay?" the driver snapped through gritted teeth.

Carter's eyes locked on the gate up ahead. Floodlights bathed the perimeter in stark white. A service checkpoint. If they could reach it—

"Just get us there," Carter said.

The Peugeot surged forward one last time, smoke curling from its hood. The Mercedes was a breath behind them when the guards at the checkpoint raised rifles and waved them down.

The Peugeot skidded to a halt.

The Mercedes slammed its brakes and turned hard—peeling away into the darkness before the guards could react.

Breathe heaving, Carter stepped out of the car, glass crunching underfoot. He didn't look back.

They had made it.

But barely.

Chapter 19: A Race Against Time

But as he stepped onto the curb, a figure emerged from the shadows near the entrance.

Solomon.

Smiling. Waiting.

"You didn't think it would be that easy, did you?"

Chapter 20: A Dangerous Proposition

Carter froze. His heart pounded as he locked eyes with Solomon, who stood casually near the terminal entrance, hands tucked into the pockets of his tailored suit. The smirk on his face sent a chill down Carter's spine.

"You're persistent," Carter said, adjusting the strap of his bag.

Solomon chuckled. "I have to be. You're a valuable man, Carter. Too valuable to let walk away so easily. " He gestured toward the entrance. "Shall we talk? "

Carter scanned the terminal doors. Crowded. Security officers milling about. He wasn't alone. That gave him a sliver of confidence.

"I have a flight to catch," he said, stepping forward.

Solomon moved with him, staying at his side. "Flights can be rescheduled. What I'm offering you is a much better deal. "

Carter clenched his jaw. "I'm done with deals."

Solomon sighed theatrically. "That's unfortunate. Because there are people inside this airport who would love to have a word with you. "

Carter's blood ran cold. He knew what Solomon meant. If he was flagged by airport security—

either real officers or men on Solomon's payroll—he wouldn't be boarding that plane.

Solomon leaned in slightly. "Here's what I propose: one last meeting. One hour. Hear me out, and then—if you still want to go—you're free to walk away."

Carter knew better than to trust him, but what choice did he have? If he forced his way through security now, he risked being detained. And once that happened, he wouldn't be walking away from anything.

One hour. One last meeting.

He exhaled slowly. "Where?"

Solomon's smirk widened. "Follow me."

Chapter 21: The Final Offer

Carter followed Solomon through the airport's bustling entrance, his every nerve on high alert. He wasn't sure if this was a trap, a negotiation, or something worse. All he knew was that he had to stay sharp if he wanted to get out of Lagos alive.

Solomon led him past the check-in counters, past the security lines, and through an unmarked door. Carter hesitated. This was the kind of door that once you stepped through, you might not come back.

"You're wasting time," Solomon said, sensing his hesitation. "And time is not something you have a lot of."

Carter exhaled sharply and stepped inside.

The room was small, dimly lit, and smelled faintly of stale cigarettes. A single table sat in the center, with two chairs facing each other. A ceiling fan spun lazily overhead. Against the far wall, another man stood—tall, broad-shouldered, and silent. Carter didn't need an introduction. He was muscle.

Solomon gestured toward the chair. "Sit."

Carter remained standing. "Say what you need to say."

Solomon sighed, took a seat himself, and laced his fingers together. "You're a businessman, Carter. And businessmen don't walk away from opportunities."

"This isn't an opportunity," Carter shot back. "It's a death wish."

Solomon chuckled. "That depends entirely on your choices." He leaned forward. "I'm offering you one last chance. Work with us. Help us finish this deal, and you leave with your five million—untouched, unbothered. But if you insist on walking away, well… let's just say, Lagos can be an unforgiving city."

Carter's gut twisted. He'd been backed into a corner before, but never like this. His mind worked furiously. Could he outmaneuver them? Trick them? Or was this truly checkmate?

He had to make a decision.

And fast.

Chapter 22: A Desperate Gamble

Carter kept his expression neutral, but inside, his mind was racing. Solomon had made his offer clear—stay in the game, or never leave Lagos at all. The air in the room felt heavier, the silence thick with unspoken threats.

He needed a way out.

Slowly, he pulled out a cigarette from his pocket, a habit he had long since quit but occasionally used as a prop. He tapped it against his palm, then looked up at Solomon.

"I don't trust you," he said flatly.

Solomon smirked. "I'd be disappointed if you did."

Carter lit the cigarette, took a slow drag, and exhaled. It gave him just enough time to formulate his next move. He needed leverage—something Solomon wanted badly enough to give him an opening.

"You said five million," Carter said. "But I don't believe that's your real number."

Solomon's eyes flickered with interest. "Go on."

Carter leaned forward, lowering his voice. "I've been around long enough to know this isn't just about repatriating funds. You're covering something up. Maybe a bigger sum. Maybe bigger players. Either way, you're in deeper than you let on. "

Solomon's smirk thinned, but he said nothing.

Carter took another drag and let the tension sit between them. "So, here's my counteroffer. You let me walk out of here, unharmed, with my name clean. And in return, I make sure your real operation stays buried. "

A flicker of hesitation crossed Solomon's face. A crack in the armor.

The silent man at the back shifted, clearly waiting for a signal.

Carter pressed on. "You and I both know if I disappear, questions will be asked. People outside of Nigeria know I'm here. You can't just make me vanish without consequences. "

Solomon exhaled through his nose, his fingers drumming against the table. He was calculating. Weighing the risks.

Finally, he spoke. "You think you're a very clever man, Carter."

Carter held his gaze. "I think I'm a man who wants to live."

Another pause. Then Solomon leaned back in his chair, a slow smile spreading across his face.

"Very well," he said. "Let's see how clever you really are."

Chapter 23: The Escape Clause

Carter kept his breathing steady as Solomon studied him, the silence between them stretching uncomfortably long. He had thrown his best gamble on the table, but now came the real test—would Solomon take the bait?

Finally, Solomon let out a low chuckle and leaned forward, resting his elbows on the table. "You're right about one thing," he said. "If something were to happen to you, it would create… complications."

Carter said nothing. He knew better than to gloat.

"But that doesn't mean I can just let you walk," Solomon continued. "Not yet." He gestured slightly with his hand, and the hulking man standing by the door stepped forward. Carter tensed, but the man simply placed a leather folder on the table and slid it toward him.

"Open it," Solomon instructed.

Carter hesitated, then flipped it open. Inside were several sheets of paper—official-looking documents with his name typed across the top. He scanned them quickly, his pulse spiking as he realized what they were.

Bank transfer records.

To his account in the Cayman Islands.

For an amount far larger than five million dollars.

Carter's mouth went dry. "What the hell is this?"

Solomon smiled. "Insurance. This document says that you, Carter Weston, willingly accepted a transfer of five million dollars in payment for your role in an international financial transaction. "

Carter's grip tightened on the pages. "This isn't real."

"Oh, but it is," Solomon said smoothly. "And if anything happens to me, or if you try to run straight to the authorities, this gets released. The story won't be that Carter Weston was an innocent businessman caught in a bad deal. No, the story will be that you were a key player in an elaborate fraud scheme. "

Carter forced himself to stay calm, but his mind was racing. This was a masterful move—Solomon wasn't just letting him go; he was binding him to the operation with a fabricated trail of evidence.

"Now," Solomon continued, standing up and buttoning his suit jacket. "You're free to leave, Carter. Catch your flight. Walk out of here untouched. But know this—your name is now tied to mine. If I go down, you go down with me. "

"When this is over," Solomon added with a knowing smile, "a new world order will take root. Those who got in early will prosper. The rest? Well... the world forgets the bystanders."

Carter stared at him, unsure if he was hearing a businessman or a zealot.

Carter swallowed hard. He was being released, but not as a free man. He was leaving Lagos with a noose around his neck.

He closed the folder, took a slow breath, and stood. "I guess that means we'll both be very careful."

Solomon's smirk returned. "That's the spirit."

Without another word, Carter turned, walking toward the door. The hallway beyond led back to the bustling airport terminal, to his flight, to what was left of his future.

But as he stepped into the crowd, he knew one thing for certain.

This wasn't over. Not by a long shot.

Chapter 24: A Shadow That Follows

Carter moved through the airport terminal with calculated ease, his outward composure betraying none of the turmoil inside. He clutched his ticket in one hand, his passport in the other, walking toward the departure gate as if nothing was amiss. But inside, his mind was a battlefield of possibilities and consequences.

Solomon had just rewritten the rules of the game. Carter wasn't leaving Lagos as a survivor—he was leaving as a man under watch, with a paper trail that could be used to destroy him at any moment.

As he passed through security, he felt a pair of eyes on him. Not just from the uniformed officers scanning passengers, but from somewhere else—somewhere unseen. He resisted the urge to look over his shoulder. Paranoia wouldn't help him now.

The PA system crackled to life, announcing the boarding call for his flight to London. Carter exhaled slowly and stepped forward, handing his ticket to the attendant. She scanned it and nodded. "Safe travels, sir."

Safe. He almost laughed at the word.

He walked down the jet bridge, stepped onto the plane, and found his seat in business class. Settling in, he glanced at the other passengers, scanning their faces. Businessmen. Tourists. A mother soothing a crying infant. Normal people, unaware of the storm Carter had just walked through.

As the plane taxied toward the runway, he allowed himself a moment of relief. He was leaving Nigeria.

But he wasn't free.

Solomon had left a mark on him, a stain that wouldn't wash away easily. He could never be sure when—or if—the other shoe would drop. If one day, a knock at his door would bring authorities holding those forged bank records. If he would wake up to a call demanding another favor, another job, another risk.

As the wheels lifted off the ground and Lagos shrank beneath him, Carter made a silent vow.

He would find a way to take back control.

This wasn't over.

Chapter 25: The Weight of a Name

Carter sat rigidly in his business-class seat, staring blankly out the window as the Atlantic stretched endlessly beneath him. The hum of the engines did little to quiet his mind. He had escaped Lagos, but he wasn't free. Solomon had made sure of that.

The flight attendant leaned in. "Would you like a drink, sir?"

He forced a polite smile. "Scotch. Neat. "

She nodded and moved on, and Carter turned his thoughts inward. He had spent decades in business, closing deals, navigating egos, and outmaneuvering competitors. But he had never been marked before—not like this. Solomon had bound his name to a fabricated crime, one that could be unsealed at any moment if Carter ever made the wrong move.

A soft chime signaled that the fasten-seatbelt sign had been turned off. He reached into his carry-on and pulled out a notepad. If he was going to fix this, he needed a plan.

First, the Cayman Islands account. He needed to verify if Solomon had actually moved money there or if the documents were purely a threat. That meant a discreet visit—no calls, no emails.

Second, leverage. Solomon held the upper hand, but Carter knew that in the world of power plays, no one was untouchable. If Solomon had gone to such lengths to control him, that meant he had his own vulnerabilities. Carter needed to find them.

And third, an exit strategy. If this situation turned worse, he needed a way to disappear. A new identity, perhaps. A country without an extradition treaty. It wasn't a move he wanted to make, but if push came to shove, he had to be ready.

The flight attendant returned, setting the scotch on his tray. Carter took a slow sip, letting the warmth settle his nerves. He glanced around the cabin again, his instincts still tingling.

Then he saw him.

A man, seated two rows back, sunglasses on despite the dim cabin lights. He wasn't reading, wasn't watching a movie—just sitting, still as a statue.

Carter felt the familiar weight of unease settle in his gut.

He was being followed.

Chapter 26: The Shadow on the Plane

Carter forced himself to remain still, swirling the amber liquid in his glass as he kept the man in his peripheral vision. He'd learned long ago that the best way to spot a tail was not to look for them—but to let them reveal themselves.

The man hadn't moved. No magazine, no book, no attempt to blend in. That was either arrogance or inexperience, and Carter wasn't sure which was worse.

He took another slow sip of his drink, then casually reached for his carry-on, pretending to adjust it beneath the seat in front of him. In the process, he glanced down the aisle and caught another detail—one that made his pulse quicken.

The man wasn't alone.

A second watcher, seated near the rear of the cabin, had the same stillness, the same feigned disinterest.

Carter exhaled through his nose. Solomon wasn't taking any chances. Either these men were insurance, making sure he didn't deviate from his flight plan, or they had a different purpose entirely.

The flight to London still had six hours to go. That was a long time to be boxed in at 35,000 feet.

Options. He needed options.

He reached into his jacket pocket, pulling out a pen and his notepad, jotting down a simple message:

"I know you're watching. Let's talk. "

He folded the page neatly, then signaled for the flight attendant. When she arrived, he gave his best weary-businessman smile. "Could you do me a favor? I think I recognize that gentleman in 7B. Would you mind passing him a note? "

She hesitated, glancing at the man, then shrugged. "I suppose."

Carter watched as she walked down the aisle and slipped the folded note onto the man's tray table.

The man didn't react immediately. He let it sit there, untouched, for almost a full minute. Then, with deliberate slowness, he picked it up, unfolded it, and read.

Then he smiled.

Not the kind of smile Carter liked.

The man reached into his jacket, pulled out a pen, and scrawled something on the same paper. He folded it again, passed it back to the flight attendant, who returned it to Carter with a polite nod.

He unfolded the page, heart pounding.

"Keep drinking. You'll need it. "

Carter exhaled sharply, his grip tightening around the note.

So, that was how this game was going to play out.

Chapter 27: Nowhere to Run

Carter stared at the note in his hand, his mind racing. The message wasn't just a warning—it was a statement of control. These men weren't here to make a move on the plane. They were here to remind him that no matter where he ran, Solomon's reach extended far beyond Lagos.

He took another sip of scotch, masking his nerves behind a calm exterior. If they wanted him to drink, he'd drink—but he wouldn't be caught off guard.

The seatbelt sign dinged on, and the captain's voice crackled over the intercom. "Ladies and gentlemen, we're approaching some turbulence. Please return to your seats and fasten your seatbelts."

Perfect.

Carter used the moment of distraction to act. He leaned forward, pretending to adjust his shoes, and slid the note under the seat cushion. If anything happened to him, someone would find it.

The plane rocked slightly as it hit the turbulence, and Carter felt the energy shift in the cabin. People murmured, a baby cried, but the two watchers remained still. They weren't nervous about the flight.

Because they weren't worried about getting to London.

They were worried about getting him to London.

Carter took a deep breath and made a decision. If Solomon wanted him to land in London that meant London was the last place he wanted to be. He needed to disappear—before they reached Heathrow.

But how?

His first-class seat didn't give him many options. Flight attendants kept a close watch on movement in and out of the cabin. He needed to think fast.

Then he remembered something—an old trick he'd once heard from a corporate spy in Bangkok.

A medical emergency.

Carter reached for his stomach and grimaced. He coughed, shifting in his seat, letting out a soft groan. Then louder. The flight attendant was at his side in moments.

"Sir, are you alright?"

Carter shook his head, breathing heavily. "I— I think it's the food. Something's wrong. My stomach—I feel faint. "

The woman frowned. "Do you need a doctor?"

He nodded weakly. "Please. I don't know if I can—" He gripped the armrest dramatically. "I think I might pass out."

The turbulence helped sell the performance. The passengers around him shifted uncomfortably, and a few craned their necks.

The attendant quickly turned toward the intercom. "If there's a medical professional onboard, please make yourself known to the crew."

That was his moment.

As attention shifted, Carter darted a glance back at his watchers. They were alert but unmoving—watching, waiting. They weren't about to make a scene on the plane.

But that meant they had a plan for him after landing.

And that meant Carter needed to make sure he never landed in London at all.

Chapter 28: An Exit at 35,000 Feet

Carter focused on controlling his breathing as the flight attendant rushed toward the galley to confer with the other crew members. The turbulence had finally subsided, but the tension inside the cabin remained thick. He could feel the eyes of his watchers burning into him, assessing whether his sudden illness was genuine—or a ploy.

It didn't matter. He only needed a few more minutes.

A middle-aged man in a crisp suit approached from the rear of the cabin, followed closely by a flight attendant. The man carried himself with authority, his expression tight with concern.

"I'm Dr. Evans," he said, kneeling beside Carter's seat. "Tell me what you're feeling."

Carter groaned, pressing a shaky hand to his forehead. "Nausea… stomach cramps… dizzy." He let his voice waver as if he were barely keeping it together. "Feels like food poisoning… or worse."

Dr. Evans placed two fingers on Carter's wrist, taking his pulse. "Your heart rate's a little fast. Any chest pain? "

Carter shook his head weakly. "No, just… something's not right." He let his head loll slightly to the side, as if his strength was fading.

The doctor frowned. "Flight attendant, we need to notify the captain. If this worsens, we may need to consider an emergency landing. "

Carter almost sighed in relief. That's it—give me an out.

The flight attendant hesitated. "A diversion would be a serious decision, doctor. We're over the Atlantic. "

"His symptoms could indicate something more severe. Dehydration or internal distress. If he collapses mid-flight, we'll regret not acting sooner. "

The flight attendant nodded and hurried off toward the cockpit.

Carter risked a glance at his watchers.

The one in 7B remained still, his hands steepled under his chin, expression unreadable. But the second man, near the back of the cabin was smiling and pounding his fist into his hand.

They were adapting. Planning their counter-move.

Carter had to stay ahead.

A moment later, the flight attendant returned. "The captain is checking for the nearest possible diversion. Stand by. "

Carter exhaled slowly, keeping up the act. He had no idea where they'd be directed—Bermuda? The Azores? He'd take anything that wasn't London.

Then the PA crackled to life.

"Ladies and gentlemen, this is your captain speaking. Due to a medical emergency, we will be making an unscheduled landing in Lisbon, Portugal. Estimated arrival in approximately 45 minutes. "

Lisbon. That could work.

Carter could already feel the frustration radiating from his watchers. Their plan had been disrupted. But they weren't out of the game yet.

And neither was he.

As the plane began its slow descent, Carter knew the real battle was just beginning.

Chapter 29: The Lisbon Gamble

Carter gripped the armrest as the plane began its descent toward Lisbon. He could feel the shift in atmosphere—not just the change in altitude, but the tightening of tension from the men watching him. His medical diversion had worked, but now came the hard part: slipping away before they adjusted their plans.

The captain's voice crackled through the intercom.

"Flight crew, prepare for landing. Medical personnel will be on standby upon arrival. "

That was a double-edged sword. On one hand, the presence of medical staff might provide cover for his exit. On the other, it meant additional security—airport personnel, customs officers, and possibly local authorities, all of whom could unknowingly assist his watchers in keeping him contained.

He needed to move fast.

The flight attendants were busy securing the cabin, which gave him a brief moment to think. He glanced at the man in 7B. The agent was calm, controlled—but there was something in his posture that told Carter he was preparing for the next step.

The moment they landed, these men would be on him.

He needed to get ahead of them.

The wheels touched down smoothly, the engines reversing as the plane slowed on the tarmac. Carter feigned another wave of dizziness, clutching his stomach and groaning loudly. The flight attendant rushed to his side.

"We've landed, sir. Medics will be boarding soon. Just stay seated. "

He nodded weakly but kept his eyes on the movement outside. A white medical van was already pulling up beside the plane, its flashing lights reflecting off the terminal windows.

The jet bridge wasn't being used. That was good—passengers would have to deplane onto the tarmac. If he could slip away in the chaos, he might have a chance.

The doors opened, and within seconds, uniformed paramedics climbed aboard. A tall man with graying hair knelt beside him, speaking in Portuguese before switching to English.

"You are unwell?"

Carter nodded. "Food poisoning. Bad cramps. Dizzy. "

The medic turned to the flight crew. "We will take him to the airport clinic for examination."

Perfect.

The paramedics lifted him to his feet, guiding him toward the front exit. As he stumbled forward, he stole a glance behind him. His watchers remained seated, outwardly calm, but their eyes followed his every move.

They weren't stopping him yet. They didn't need to.

They knew exactly where he was going.

Carter stepped onto the metal stairs leading down to the tarmac, the humid Lisbon air hitting his face. The medical team helped him toward the waiting van. He climbed inside, settling onto the stretcher.

The doors shut. The driver shifted into gear.

Then, just as they began rolling forward, Carter made his move.

He sprang from the stretcher, lunging for the rear doors. The medics shouted in confusion, but before they could react, he threw the latch and leapt out onto the pavement.

Pain jolted through his knees as he hit the ground. He rolled, scrambled to his feet, and sprinted.

Behind him, he heard shouting. Footsteps. The agents were coming.

But Carter had one advantage—they hadn't expected him to run now.

And he wasn't planning on stopping.

Chapter 30: Running for His Life

Carter's feet pounded against the tarmac as he sprinted toward the nearest terminal entrance. His heart thundered in his chest, adrenaline fueling his escape. Behind him, shouts rang out—Portuguese airport security, flight crew, and most importantly, the men Solomon had sent to watch him.

He risked a glance over his shoulder.

The two watchers were now in motion, breaking into a run. They had been expecting him to stay in the care of the medical team, to be guided neatly into their trap. His escape had thrown them off, but not enough to stop them.

Ahead, the airport terminal loomed, its automatic glass doors reflecting the glow of fluorescent lights. He had one shot at making it inside before security locked things down.

A uniformed officer near the entrance spotted the commotion and raised a hand, calling out in Portuguese. Carter didn't stop. He charged forward, panting.

"Help! They're chasing me! " he shouted, hoping the officer would react on instinct.

The guard's brow furrowed in confusion, but Carter didn't wait for a response. He bolted through the doors, shoving past startled travelers. The terminal was a maze of kiosks, departure boards, and baggage carousels.

Think, Carter, think.

He needed to disappear, to blend in. The agents chasing him weren't about to pull weapons in a crowded airport, but they wouldn't stop hunting him either.

He scanned the terminal. To the left—passport control, too risky. Straight ahead—escalators leading to an upper-level food court. To the right—restrooms, an emergency exit, and... a row of airline service counters.

His eyes locked onto a lone ticket agent behind the Air France desk.

Carter made a beeline for it.

"Excuse me," he gasped, slapping his passport onto the counter. "I need to book a last-minute flight. Now. "

The woman behind the counter blinked in surprise but recovered quickly. "Where to, sir?"

"Anywhere that boards in the next twenty minutes."

She hesitated. "That's very short notice—"

Carter pulled a hundred-dollar bill from his pocket and slid it across the counter. "Please. It's urgent. "

The woman's eyes flicked between him and the money. Then she began typing.

Behind him, Carter caught a glimpse of his pursuers pushing through the crowd. His time was running out.

The agent's fingers moved swiftly over the keyboard. "There's a flight to Casablanca departing in fifteen minutes. One seat left in business class. "

"I'll take it."

She printed the boarding pass. Carter snatched it, grabbed his passport, and turned—just as his pursuers spotted him.

They started toward him.

Carter spun on his heel and bolted toward security. If he could just get past the checkpoint, onto the jet bridge, into the plane—

Then, maybe, he'd live to fight another day.

Chapter 31: A Narrow Escape

Carter weaved through the terminal crowd, his pulse hammering as he made a beeline for the security checkpoint. The Air France ticket agent had given him his golden ticket—now he just had to get through screening before his pursuers caught up.

Behind him, he caught a glimpse of the two agents closing in, pushing past startled travelers with ruthless efficiency. They weren't running yet, not wanting to cause a scene, but their eyes were locked on him.

Carter reached the security line and forced himself to slow down, blending into the queue of passengers shuffling toward the metal detectors. He slid off his jacket, placed his carry-on in the tray, and did his best to look like just another business traveler in a rush.

The agent at the conveyor belt barely glanced at him as he stepped through the scanner. A quick beep, then a nod. He was through.

Grabbing his bag, he moved toward the terminal corridor—just as he saw one of the agents stepping into the security line. The other was hanging back, speaking urgently into his phone.

They're adapting. Calling ahead.

Carter pushed forward, scanning for signs to his gate. The flight to Casablanca was boarding at Gate 34—down a long concourse, just past a duty-free shop. He kept moving, resisting the urge to run. Running would draw attention. Running would tell them he knew he was trapped.

Stay calm. Act like you belong.

Gate 34 came into view. The final boarding call was flashing on the screen. Passengers were trickling onto the jet bridge.

Carter reached the desk and handed over his boarding pass. The gate agent scanned it, gave him a polite nod, and motioned him through.

He exhaled slowly, stepping onto the jet bridge. Almost there.

As he neared the plane's entrance, a sinking feeling gripped him. His pursuers weren't fools. They knew where he was going. Would they be waiting for him in Casablanca? Had they already made a call to Moroccan authorities?

For now, all that mattered was getting on this plane and into the air. He stepped into the cool, controlled air of the cabin, flashing a tense smile at the flight attendants.

Taking his seat in business class, he buckled in, willing himself to relax.

The engines hummed to life. The doors sealed.

And as the plane taxied down the runway, Carter dared to believe—for the first time in hours— that he might just survive the night.

Chapter 32: – The Call for Help

As Carter's flight cruised at 35,000 feet toward Casablanca, he knew he couldn't land blind. Lagos had been a disaster, and there was no telling who might be waiting for him on the ground. Every move now had to be calculated; every decision precise.

He scrolled through his phone, hesitating before selecting a familiar name: Tom Leland.

A seasoned expatriate with connections across Africa and Europe, Leland was the kind of man who knew things—who heard whispers before they became headlines. If anyone could give Carter a lay of the land before touchdown, it was him.

Carter tapped the call button. The line rang twice before a gruff voice answered.

"You better have a good reason for this, Carter."

Carter exhaled. "Tom, I need eyes in Casablanca. Are you still tapped in? "

A pause. Then, "Depends. Who's looking for you? "

Carter glanced around the dimly lit cabin, lowering his voice. "More people than I can count. Nigeria was a trap, and I don't know if Morocco's any better. "

Tom sighed. "Damn it, Carter. I told you that deal smelled badly. "

"Yeah, well, you were right."

Another pause. Then Tom's voice softened just slightly. "Alright. I'll make some calls. But listen—if I tell you to divert, you do it. No arguments. "

Carter nodded to himself. "Understood."

A minute later, a message popped up on Carter's phone:

Tariq El Mansour. +212 655 44 3219. Good Luck.

Carter stared at the name. He didn't know whether it was a lifeline or another door into deeper trouble. Either way, he didn't have a choice.

Chapter 33: Meeting Tariq

Carter's plane touched down at Mohammed V International Airport just after sunset. The humid air clung to him as he stepped off the jet way, his carry-on slung over his shoulder. He moved quickly through customs, keeping his head down, hoping that whatever trouble was following him from Lagos hadn't beaten him here.

His phone buzzed as he exited the terminal. A message from Tariq El-Mansour:

"Café Al-Kabir. 20 minutes. Come alone."

Carter glanced around, scanning for any sign of surveillance. He spotted a line of black sedans parked along the curb, their drivers leaning against their hoods, watching the steady stream of passengers with practiced indifference. His instincts told him not to linger.

He hailed a taxi and gave the driver the address Tariq had sent. The cab sped off, weaving through the congested Casablanca streets. The city pulsed with life—street vendors shouting in Arabic and French, neon lights flickering over weathered shopfronts, the scent of grilled meat and spices wafting through the open window.

Fifteen minutes later, the taxi pulled up in front of Café Al-Kabir, a dimly lit spot tucked between a butcher shop and a cigarette vendor. Carter paid the driver and stepped onto the sidewalk.

Inside, the café was nearly empty. A few men huddled over small glasses of mint tea, speaking in hushed tones. In the far corner, a man in his late forties sat alone, stirring his coffee. He wore a well-tailored navy suit, his salt-and-pepper beard neatly trimmed. He didn't look up as Carter approached.

Carter slid into the chair across from him. "Tariq?"

The man stirred his coffee once more before setting the spoon down. He lifted his gaze, dark eyes assessing Carter with quiet intensity.

"You're late," Tariq said.

Carter smirked. "The plane was on time. I'm exactly where I need to be. "

Tariq exhaled through his nose, unimpressed. He reached into his jacket and slid a small envelope across the table. Carter hesitated before picking it up. Inside were two forged Moroccan identity cards—one with his real face, one with a slightly altered version.

"That will get you around the city," Tariq said. "But not forever. If someone serious is after you, they will know these are fake. "

"Noted," Carter said. "I just need enough time to get out of here in one piece."

Tariq leaned back. "Then you better tell me— who is after you, and why should I help you?"

Carter hesitated, choosing his words carefully. "Let's just say some powerful people want something I don't have. And they don't take 'no' for an answer. "

Tariq sighed. "Your friend at the State Department asked me for a favor. That's the only reason we're talking. But favors don't come free. "

Carter nodded. He expected this. "How much?"

Tariq took a slow sip of his coffee before setting it down. "Not money. I need something done. You do it, and I'll make sure you leave Casablanca alive. "

Carter tensed. He wasn't sure what was worse—handing over a briefcase full of cash or owing a man like Tariq a favor.

But he was out of options.

"What do you need?" Carter asked.

Tariq's lips curled into the faintest hint of a smile.

"Let's take a walk," he said.

Chapter 34: The Favor

Carter followed Tariq through the winding streets of Casablanca's old medina, his senses on high alert. The narrow alleys were alive with movement—vendors haggling, children darting past, the scent of grilled lamb and fresh bread filling the night air. Tariq walked with purpose, his steps confident, as if he had done this a thousand times before.

After several turns, they arrived at a discrete doorway set into the side of a weathered building. Tariq knocked twice, then once more after a pause. A moment later, the door creaked open, revealing a young man in his twenties, his sharp eyes scanning Carter before stepping aside to let them in.

The room was small, dimly lit by a single overhead bulb. A desk sat in the corner, cluttered with maps and documents. On the far side of the room, a battered leather chair was occupied by an older man with a neatly trimmed mustache. His dark suit, though slightly worn, suggested an air of authority.

"This is Hamid," Tariq said, gesturing to the man in the chair. "He has a problem. You are going to help him solve it. "

Carter crossed his arms, "that depends on the problem."

Hamid studied Carter for a long moment before speaking. "There is a man in the city. A former intelligence officer turned businessman. He has something that belongs to me. A file—one that

contains information that I cannot allowed to be used.
"

Carter's jaw tightened. He had played enough games like this to know that 'information' usually meant leverage, and leverage meant danger.

"You want me to steal it?" he asked. Hamid's lips curled onto a slight smile. "You're quick. Yes. But let's not call it stealing, let's call it…retrieval. "

Carter exhaled. "Where is it?"

Tariq answered this time. "The man keeps an office near the port. He's careful—rarely leaves anything of value unguarded. But he has a meeting tomorrow night at the Grand Atlantic Hotel. That will be your window"

Carter frowned. "Why not send one of your own men?"

Hamid's expression darkened slightly. "If I could, I would. But I am being watched—closely. The moment any of my people make a move, it will be noticed. You, on the other hand, are an outsider. You have the advantage of surprise. "

Carter weighed his options. This wasn't a favor—this was a job. A risky one. But if it meant securing his exit from Casablanca, he had no choice.

He glanced at Tariq. "And if I do this, you get me out of here?

Tariq nodded. "Clean papers. Safe passage. But you need to move quickly. "

Carter sighed, rubbing his temples. "Fine. Give me the details. "

Hamid leaned forward, placing a small folder on the table. "Everything you to know is in here. Do not fail. " Carter took the folder, already regretting his decision. But there was no turning back now.

Tariq clapped him on the shoulder. "Good luck my friend. You'll need it. "

Chapter 35: The Heist

Carter spent the next few hours studying the contents of the folder. The target, Anton Rinaldi, was an Italian national with ties to intelligence circles. His office, located in a nondescript building near the Casablanca port, was protected by a state-of-the-art security system and at least two armed guards. The file Carter needed was stored in a safe, and according to Hamid, Rinaldi never left it unattended—except during meetings like the one he had scheduled for tomorrow night.

The plan was simple in theory: wait for Rinaldi to leave, get inside, crack the safe, and disappear. But in practice, it was anything but.

Carter spent the next day preparing. He secured a stolen access card from a street contact Tariq had arranged and scouted the office location. The building had two exits, one heavily guarded, the other an emergency fire escape with an outdated lock—his best bet for an easy exit.

As night fell, he dressed in dark clothing, strapped a small toolkit to his belt, and set off toward the port. The city streets buzzed with life, but Carter's focus was razor-sharp. By the time he reached Rinaldi's office, he had already mapped his route in his mind.

A quick glance at his watch. 9:17 PM. Right on schedule.

From a shadowed alley, Carter watched as Rinaldi exited the building, flanked by two men. They climbed into a black sedan and disappeared into the night.

Showtime.

Carter moved swiftly, approaching the side door. The stolen access card slid through the reader, and for a tense second, he thought it wouldn't work. Then—click—the lock released. He slipped inside.

The office was silent, the hum of an air conditioning unit the only sound. Carter navigated through the dimly lit corridors, reaching Rinaldi's private office within minutes. He pulled the door shut behind him and turned to face the safe.

A high-end model. Digital keypad, biometric scanner. No easy way in.

Carter exhaled sharply, thinking fast. He had no fancy hacking device—just his instincts and whatever he could improvise. He pulled open the desk drawers, searching for anything useful. A notepad, loose change, a pen. Nothing helpful.

Then he spotted it—a smudge on the biometric scanner. Faint, but visible under the glow of the desk lamp. Carter reached into his pocket, pulling out a small tube of lip balm he had swiped earlier from the hotel room. He dabbed a thin layer over the scanner and pressed his thumb against it, hoping to transfer the faint print left behind.

The lock beeped. Processing...

For a moment, nothing happened. Then, with a soft click, the safe unlocked.

Carter let out a slow breath. He wasn't a hacker, but sometimes, all you needed was a little improvisation.

He pulled the door open and grabbed the file. Flipping through it, he saw classified reports, financial records, and—

His breath caught.

A photograph of himself. Dated before he had even set foot in Casablanca.

He wasn't just stealing information.

Someone had been watching him all along.

A noise in the hallway. Carter snapped the file shut and shoved it inside his jacket. No time for second-guessing. He bolted toward the fire escape, praying his luck would hold.

Tonight, he was playing for his life.

Chapter 36: A Narrow Escape

Carter's heartbeat thundered in his chest as he bolted toward the fire escape. He could hear footsteps in the hallway now—sharp, hurried. Someone had noticed the breach.

He reached the window, unlatched it, and swung a leg over just as the office door burst open. A harsh voice shouted in Italian. Carter didn't wait to translate. He dropped onto the fire escape, landing with a metallic clang that sent an echo through the alleyway below.

A gunshot rang out. The bullet slammed into the metal railing inches from his shoulder, sending up a spray of sparks. Carter cursed and took the stairs three at a time, his muscles burning as he descended toward the alley.

More shouts, more footsteps. He was running out of time.

He hit the ground and sprinted. The streets of Casablanca blurred around him as he dodged past pedestrians and ducked into the shadows of a narrow street. He needed distance—needed a way to shake whoever was on his tail.

Ahead, a fruit vendor was packing up for the night. Carter yanked the hood of his jacket over his head and slowed to a brisk walk. A quick glance over his shoulder—two men in dark suits emerged from the alley he had just escaped from, scanning the crowd.

Carter grabbed a crate of oranges from the vendor's cart and shoved a few bills into the man's hand. "Sorry, I need this."

Before the vendee could protest, Carter spun and tossed the crate into the path of his pursuers. Oranges exploded across the cobblestones', sending bystanders scrambling. The distraction bought him just enough time ti disappears around the corner.

Breathing hard, he kept moving, zigzagging through the streets until he spotted a familiar landmark—the neon glow of a small café where he and had agreed to meet Tariq.

He slipped inside, the bell above the door jingling softly. The place was nearly empty. Tariq sat in a booth at the back, sipping mint tea, his expression unreadable. Carter slid into the seat across from him and pulled the stolen file from his jacket. "We have a problem."

Tariq's gaze flicked to the file, then back to Carter. "I assume this means you got what we needed.

Carter exhaled sharply. "I got more than that." He opened the file and pointed to the photo of himself. "They knew I saws coming. They've always been watching me.

Tariq's jaw tightened. "Then we need to move. Now. "

Carter nodded. Whatever was happening, it was bigger than he had realized. And if he didn't get out of Casablanca soon, he might not get out at all.

Chapter 37: Nowhere to Hide

Carter and Tariq slipped out of the café through the back entrance, moving quickly but without drawing attention. The streets were alive with the usual nighttime energy of Casablanca, but Carter felt an undercurrent of danger in every shadow. He knew the men who had been following him wouldn't stop now. If anything, they would tighten the net.

Tariq led him through of alleyways, taking an indirect rout toward an old garage he used as a safe house. It was a risk, but they needed a place to regroup.

Inside the dimly lit space, Tariq locked the heavy metal door behind them. "We don't have much time. If they had your photo they had a plan. "

Carter ran his hand through his hair, exhaling sharply. "They were ahead of me every step of the way. Someone tipped them off. "

Tariq nodded grimly. "There are only a few people who knew you were coming for that file."

Carter's mind raced through the possibilities. Solomon? No, he had more to gain if Carter succeeded. Hamid? Maybe. Or had his former State Department contact unknowingly compromised him?

Tariq crossed the room, retrieving an old radio transceiver from a shelf. "No phones. Too easy to track. If you need to get word to someone, this is the best we can do. "

Carter frowned. "And who exactly would I call?"

Tariq hesitated, then shrugged. "Then we do it the hard way. There's a ship leaving the harbor at dawn. A freighter—no questions asked. It can get you as far as Gibraltar. "

Carter clenched his jaw. "And from there?"

"Call this number when you arrive."

Carter exhaled, glancing around the cramped garage. The walls smelled of oil and rust, the air thick with the scent of old metal. There was no backup coming, no cavalry. It was just him.

Tariq checked his watch. "We leave in ten minutes."

Carter met his eyes. "Then let's move."

Chapter 38: The Escape Route

Carter adjusted the collar of his jacket and followed Tariq through the labyrinthine streets of Casablanca. The air smelled of salt and diesel as they neared the port. Every shadow seemed alive, every passerby a potential threat. He forced himself to stay calm.

Tariq led him to a side street, where an old Peugeot idled by the curb. A burly man in a worn leather jacket stepped out, nodding once to Tariq. "This him?"

Tariq gestured toward Carter. "Yes Omar, meet our friend. He's in need of passage. "

Omar grunted and motioned for Carter to get in. "The ship leaves in less than an hour. If we don't make it, you're on your own. "

Carter climbed into the backseat, Tariq taking the front. The car rumbled to life and they sped toward the harbor. The streets were quieter now, the city settling into its late-night lull. But Carter knew better than to assume they weren't being watched.

As they neared the docks, Omar took a sudden turn down an alley and killed the headlights. "We walk from here," he said. "Less attention."

Carter stepped out, scanning the surroundings. A cargo freighter loomed ahead; its deck lights casting long reflections on the water. Crew members moved about, securing the last of the cargo.

Tariq handed Carter a small dog-eared passport. "New name, new identity. Memorize it."

Carter flipped through it. His face, but a different name. He exhaled. "This will get me aboard?"

Omar smirked. "If anyone askes, you're a deckhand. Just keep your head down."

They made their way to the loading ramp. Omar whispered something to a dockworker, slipping him a folded note. The man hesitated, then nodded, motioning them forward.

Carter was halfway up the ramp when a shout rang out behind them. He turned just in time to see two men in suits rounding the corner, guns drawn,

"Go!" Tariq barked, shoving Carter forward.

Carter sprinted up the ramp as bullets cracked against metal. Crew members scattered. He dove behind a crate just as the ship's horn bellowed—a signal that departure was imminent.

Tariq fired off two quick shots, forcing their pursuers to take cover. "Get below deck!" he shouted.

Carter didn't/t need to be told twice. He dashed through a side door, disappearing into a maze of corridors. He was on board. Now, he just had to stay alive long enough to reach Gibraltar.

Chapter 39: Into the Unknown

Carter pressed himself against the cold steel wall of the ship's narrow corridor, listing for footsteps. The ship vibrated beneath him as the engines roared to life, pulling away from the Casablanca port. He had made it on board—but so had his enemies.

The sound of hurried boots echoed down the companionway. He had seconds to act. Spotting an open hatch, he slipped inside, closing it behind him. The room was dark, filled with stacked crates and the scent of salt and oil. He crouched low, forcing himself to control his breathing.

The door handle rattled.

Carter's heart pounded. A flashlight beam sliced through the narrow gap beneath the door. A voice muttered something in Arabic. The handle giggled again, then stopped. The footsteps retreated.

He exhaled slowly. Not safe yet.

Moving quickly, he scanned the room. A small maintenance ladder led up to what looked like an access hatch. He climbed, pushing the hatch open just enough to peek through. Above, the deck stretched out beneath the night sky, waves crashing against the hull.

Slipping through, crouched low and scanned for threats. Crew members moved about oblivious to his presence. But he knew the men from the docks would' stop hunting him.

He needed a plan.

A shadow moved near the bridge. He recognized the shape instantly—one of his pursuers, sweeping the deck with a pistol in hand.

Carter ducked behind a lifeboat, mind racing. He had made it this far, but Gibraltar was still hours away. If he wanted to survive, he had to turn the game around.

And he had to do it fast.

Chapter 40: The Turning Tide

Carter remained crouched behind the lifeboat, his mind working through possible escape routes. The ship was moving steadily through the dark waters of the Atlantic, bound for Gibraltar, but his pursuers were still on board. He had to act before they closed in.

A crew member walked past, whistling softly, oblivious to the danger lurking on deck. Carter seized the opportunity. He stepped out and fell into stride behind the man, mimicking his relaxed pace. The key was to blend in.

As he neared the supply room, he caught sift of one of the suited men scanning the deck. Carter ducked inside just as the man turned his head in his direction. He held his breath, waiting for any sign he'd been seen.

Silence.

He exhaled and turned to survey the room. Stacked provisions, toolboxes, and rows of orange work jumpsuits. Perfect.

He grabbed a jumpsuit and pulled it on over his cloths, then slipped a crew cap low over his forehead. With luck, it would buy him enough time.

His stolen jumpsuit smelled of sweat and machine oil, but it helped him blend in. The crew cap covered his face, and he kept his head down as he moved through the cramped passageways. He just needed to stay out of sight for the first leg of the journey.

Then he'd make his move.

Gibraltar was still two days away. If Carter didn't find a secure hiding spot, he'd be discovered long before then. And if they figured out that he wasn't just some lost dockworker?

The clang of approaching footsteps sent Carter pressing into the shadows. A thickset crewman in a grease-streaked uniform appeared at the far end of the corridor, a clipboard tucked under one arm. His sharp eyes swept the hallway, landing right where Carter was crouched.

"Hey! You there! "

Carter's pulse kicked up. Think fast.

He straightened, wiping imaginary sweat from his brow, and forced a weary sigh. "Yeah?" he grunted, making his accent rougher.

The crewman frowned. "Who are you? I don't recognize you. "

Carter patted his jumpsuit as if looking for an ID badge. "New guy. They told me to check the lower storage—see if we're stocked for the next run. "

The crewman squinted. He was buying it— almost.

"Who told you that?"

Carter felt the blood drain from his face.

Before he could answer, a loud crack echoed from above—someone had dropped a heavy crate. The crewman turned his head for just a second. That was all Carter needed. He pivoted and slipped around the corner, moving fast but not fast enough to look like he was running.

Behind him, the crewman called out. "Hey! Wait a sec—! "

Carter ducked through a metal door and yanked it shut behind him. He was in a storage bay, surrounded by crates, barrels and crew provisions for the voyage to Gibraltar. No way out. His only chance now was hiding.

His eyes scanned the storage room. There—a maintenance hatch leading to the ship's ventilation system. Tight quarters, but it might just keep him hidden.

He climbed onto a crate, pried the vent open, and wriggled inside. The metal was freezing against his skin, but it was safe—for now.

As the ship sailed deeper into open water, Carter knew one thing: he was running out of time.

And when time ran out, he'd have to fight his way free.

He didn't want to think about that.

The ship/s horn sounded, signaling a course adjustment to the Gibraltar harbor. Carter used the distraction to slip back onto the deck, keeping to the shadows. The wind howled around him, the scent of salt, heavy in the air.

Time to leave the ship.

He spotted an open door leading to the engine room. If he could disable the ships power for even a few minutes, it might give him the upper hand.

He moved quickly, descending a metal staircase into the depths of the vessel. The heat was oppressive, the sound of machinery drowning out any approaching footsteps. Carter found the control panel and scanned it. He didn't have to shut down the whole ship—just cause enough of a disruption to create an opening.

His fingers moved over the switches. A moment later, the ship lurched, the lights flickering. Shouts rang out above. He gritted his teeth and sprinted back up the stairs. He had seconds before someone realized what had happened.

Back on deck, he spotted the suited man from before, now barking orders into a handheld radio. Carter knew this was his chance.

With the chaos unfolding, he made his move—heading straight for the lifeboats. It was time to leave this ship behind.

Chapter 41: Adrift in the Dark

Carter crouched near the lifeboat, heart pounding as the ship's lights flickered ominously. The controlled chaos on deck worked in his favor—crew members scrambled to investigate the power failure, and his pursuers were momentarily distracted. He had a window, but it was closing fast.

He gripped the control lever, hesitating for only a moment. Dropping into the ocean at night was a risk, but staying aboard was worse. With one swift motion, he yanked the lever. The small craft groaned as it disengaged, the inflatable raft slapping against the churning water below.

No time to second-guess. He swung leg over the railing and pushed off, plunging into the icy darkness.

The saltwater hit him like a fist, knocking the breath from his lungs. He fought against the undertow, reaching for the lifeboat. The ship loomed above him, its deck lights casting eerier beams across the waves.

Carter scrambled aboard the raft and pulled the starter cord on the small outboard motor. It sputtered once, then roared to life. He turned the throttle and veered away from the ship, keeping low to avoid detection. Behind him, voices shouted, flashlights scanning the water. He clenched his jaw and kept moving.

Minutes passed like hours. The ship grew smaller in the distance, its towering silhouette fading against the night sky. Carter steered toward the East, hoping to make it to the rocky shores of Gibraltar by sunrise.

The adrenaline wore off, and exhaustion set in. He was alone now, in the open sea. But he was alive. And as long as he had that, he had a chance.

He pressed forward; the distant glow of civilization barely visible on the horizon. The chase wasn't over—not yet—but for the first time in days, Carter felt something close to hope.

Chapter 42: The Escape

Carter steered the small boat toward the distant glow of Gibraltar's coastline. The hum of the engine was steady, but his thoughts raced. He had escaped the clutches of Lagos, but the danger still lingered like a shadow. As he navigated the dark waters, he clutched the one thing that made the risk worthwhile—a small, encrypted flash drive concealed beneath the lining of his watch. The digital backup contained every document, signature, and transfer record—undeniable proof of the conspiracy.

The briefcase, once an essential prop for his cover, had served its purpose. Before leaving, Carter had destroyed its contents, making it worthless to anyone who would try to track him. The real evidence was safely in his possession, digitized and ready to be exposed.

The cove came into view, its jagged cliff's shielding the small inlet. Carter throttled down, the engine sputtering softly as he approached. The plan was simple: land under the cover of night, make his way to the docks, and disappear into the narrow streets of Gibraltar. He pulled the boat closer, scanning for any signs of movement. The air was thick with the salty scent of the sea. The only sounds were the rhythmic slap of the water against the hull and the distant hum of a cargo ship far offshore.

With a deep breath, Carter cut the engine. The boat glided into the shadows of the cove. He knew that once he set foot on shore, he'd be vulnerable. But with the flash drive secure, at least the evidence would remain intact—even if he didn't.

Chapter 43: A Safe Harbor?

Carter stepped onto the dock in Gibraltar, the salty breeze cutting through the tension that had gripped him for days. He took a deep breath, inhaling fraught with uncertainty the scent of the sea, grateful to be on solid ground. His journey here had been, but at least for the moment, he was in a place where he could think clearly.

He needed to call the contact number Tariq had given him.

The contact had arranged a meeting at a small café near the marina. The establishment was quiet, tucked away from the bustling tourist areas, providing a discreet setting for their conversation. As Carter approached, he spotted a familiar face—his contact, Daniel Foster, a former international trade consultant with deep ties to both European and African markets.

Daniel greeted him with a firm handshake. "Carter, you look like hell. When I got your message, I figured something big was happening. What's going on? "

Carter sat down, glancing around to make sure no one was paying them any undue attention. "Let's just say I found myself in deeper than I expected. Nigeria was a disaster. I barely got out. Now, I need to figure out my next move before certain people start looking for me. "

Daniel nodded, signaling the waiter for two espressos. "I've heard whispers about a deal gone bad. Word travels fast in our circles. How much trouble are you in? "

Carter exhaled slowly. "Enough. I need a place to regroup, assess my options. And most importantly, I need to know who I can still trust. "

Daniel studied him for a moment before responding. "You're in Gibraltar, which means you're not out of the game just yet. But if you want my advice, lay low for a while. I might know someone who can help you disappear—at least until things cool down. "

Carter leaned in, his mind racing. He wasn't ready to disappear, not yet. But he needed a plan. And fast.

Chapter 44: A Fragile Refuge

Leaving Foster, Carter moved quickly through the dimly lit streets of Gibraltar. His wet clothes clung to him, the saltwater drying against his skin. The harbor was now a distant memory, but the fear lingered. Every passing stranger, every shadowed doorway, felt like a potential threat.

He had one goal: reach the small inn tucked along the outskirts of town. It was a place recommended by his contact—simple, discreet, and most importantly, off the radar. The kind of establishment where no one asked questions.

The streets were narrow, twisting through old stone buildings that bore the weight of centuries. Carter's mind raced with each step. The encrypted flash drive, concealed safely in his watch, was all that stood between him and the ruthless men determined to silence him. But it also held the power to expose them.

He approached the inn's weathered door and knocked twice. After a moment, a small window slid open. A pair of tired eyes examined him.

"Rooms paid for," Carter said, his voice low.

The latch clicked. The door opened just enough for him to slip inside.

"Second floor. End of the hall, "the man grunted, before locking the door behind him.

The room was sparse, with a narrow bed and a small table. Heavy curtains blocked the view of the street below. Carter tossed his soaked jacket over the chair and collapsed onto the bed, exhaustion washing over him. But even as his body ached for rest, his mind refused to settle.

He pulled the watch from his wrist, inspecting it carefully. The flash drive remained intact. Carter knew that getting the data to his contact would be the next battle. The encrypted files were his only weapon now.

Outside, the hum of distant voices and occasional footsteps reminded him that the streets were never truly empty. But for now, within these four walls, he had a fragile refuge.

Tomorrow, the chase would resume. But tonight, Carter allowed himself a rare moment of stillness.

Chapter 45: The Man in the Shadows

Carter paced along the marina, the evening breeze offering little relief from the weight pressing down on his mind. He had spent the past few weeks reacting—dodging threats, escaping danger, and trying to stay one step ahead. Now, for the first time, he was choosing to confront the unknown rather than flee from it.

Daniel had arranged the meeting with Vincent Leclerc for midnight at a secluded rooftop bar overlooking the Rock of Gibraltar. It was a strange setting for a clandestine conversation, but Carter knew better than to question a man like Leclerc's methods. If this ex-intelligence operative had agreed to see him, it meant Leclerc already knew more about his situation than Carter was comfortable with.

As the clock neared twelve, Carter made his way through the dimly lit streets, arriving at the rooftop entrance where a discreet but well-armed doorman gave him an once-over before stepping aside. The bar was nearly empty—just a few patrons scattered at distant tables, speaking in hushed tones.

At the far end of the terrace, a man sat alone, his silhouette partially obscured by the flickering glow of a candle. He was tall, lean, and had the kind of presence that made people uneasy without knowing why. His steel-gray eyes locked onto Carter the moment he entered.

"Mr. Weston," Leclerc said, gesturing for him to sit. "You've been making quite a mess."

Carter took the seat across from him, keeping his expression neutral. "I could say the same about the people chasing me."

Leclerc smirked, swirling the amber liquid in his glass. "And yet, you're still alive. That tells me you're either very good or very lucky. "

"I'd rather be smart," Carter replied. "Which is why I'm here."

Leclerc leaned back, studying him. "You're not the first businessman to get caught in a web like this. Nigeria is a playground for opportunists, con men, and those who operate in the shadows. But your case—" he paused, tapping a finger against his glass, "—your case is different. Someone went to great lengths to lure you in. That suggests you were either a target from the beginning or you stumbled into something much bigger than a simple financial scam. "

Carter stiffened. "What are you saying?"

Leclerc exhaled slowly. "I'm saying your problem isn't just the men you left behind in Lagos. It's whoever they answer to. "

Carter's pulse quickened. "And who is that?"

Leclerc gave a thin smile. "That, Mr. Weston, is what I intend to find out."

Chapter 46: Calculated Moves

Carter sat in the dim confines of the rented flat, the small space a far cry from the bustling streets of Gibraltar outside. The room was cluttered with remnants of takeout meals and empty water bottles. Sleep had eluded him for the past two nights, the hum of adrenaline refusing to subside. The encrypted flash drive, concealed in his watch, felt heavier with each passing hour.

He knew the window for action was closing. The men pursuing him were not the kind to lose track of their prey for long. Every step Carter took had to be deliberate. His mind ran through the options. He could attempt to contact his State Department friend again — a calculated risk, but one that might provide him with a lifeline. The flash drive held undeniable evidence, and if placed in the right hands, it could dismantle the entire corrupt operation.

The phone buzzed, vibrating against the scratched wooden table. Carter's heart lurched as he checked the screen. It was a secure message from his contact, confirming that a discreet meeting had been arranged. The location: a café on the edge of town, away from prying eyes.

"One hour," the message read.

Carter exhaled sharply. The plan was in motion. He stashed the watch in his pocket, grabbed his jacket, and left the flat without a backward glance.

The streets were alive with tourists and locals, the bright Mediterranean sun casting a golden hue over the limestone walls. Carter moved purposefully, avoiding eye contact and scanning for anything out of the ordinary. Despite the clear skies, a storm of uncertainty loomed over him.

At the café, he chose a corner table, positioning himself with a clear view of the entrance. Minutes passed, each one stretching endlessly. Then, a figure appeared — a woman in her mid-forties, dressed in casual attire that did little to mask her professional demeanor. She approached without hesitation, sliding into the seat across from him.

"Mr. Weston," she said, her voice low. "You've stirred up quite the situation."

"That wasn't exactly the plan," Carter replied, forcing a small smile.

She leaned forward; her eyes sharp. "You have the evidence?"

Carter tapped his pocket. "Right here. But I want assurances. I'm not walking away from this empty-handed."

"You'll get your assurances," she replied. "But first, we need to see what you've got."

He hesitated for a moment before placing the watch on the table. The woman nodded, signaling that the next phase was already in motion. As she reached for the device, Carter couldn't shake the feeling that the stakes had never been higher.

Chapter 47: Crossing the Threshold

Carter watched as the woman carefully pocketed the flash drive from the hidden compartment in his watch. Her practiced movements and calm demeanor confirmed what he suspected — she was no stranger to high-stakes operations.

"We'll analyze it immediately," she said, her gaze unwavering. "But you need to keep moving. The people after you won't stop just because we have this."

Carter nodded. "I didn't expect them to."

"You have options," she continued. "But every one of them comes with risks. We can extract you, set you up in a safe house, but even that won't guarantee you're in the clear. "

He shook his head. "I'm not hiding. I want to see this through. Solomon and his network need to be exposed."

A flicker of approval crossed her face. "Good. But that means we have to stay ahead of them. Our analysts will verify what you've given us, and once it checks out, we'll move forward. "

Carter stood, adjusting his jacket. "How long will that take?"

"Hours, not days," she assured him. "Stay off the grid. We'll be in touch. "

With that, she disappeared into the bustling street, leaving Carter alone with the weight of his decision. He felt a surge of relief knowing the evidence was now in capable hands. Still, the knowledge that Solomon's network would retaliate kept him on edge.

The Mediterranean breeze blew through the narrow alleyways as Carter made his way back toward the flat. He rehearsed his next moves, knowing that any misstep could be his last. Just as he rounded a corner, his phone vibrated. Another encrypted message.

"They're on the move. Stay low. Trust no one.
"

The words hit him like a punch to the gut.

He ducked into a nearby café, scanning the faces of the patrons as he ordered a coffee he had no intention of drinking. Every unfamiliar glance, every shadow across the window set his nerves on edge. He checked the exits, calculating how quickly he could disappear if necessary.

Minutes passed. Then a familiar figure emerged outside — Solomon's right-hand man, Kamal. His sharp eyes scanned the street, clearly searching for something — or someone.

Carter's pulse quickened. He kept his head down, pretending to check his phone. Kamal lingered just long enough to send a chill through Carter's spine before walking on.

It was a warning. They were closing in.

But Carter was done running.

Chapter 48: Closing In

Carter remained seated in the café, his mind racing as Kamal disappeared down the street. Every instinct told him to run, but running wouldn't solve anything. He'd come too far. The flash drive was in safe hands, but that didn't mean he was.

His phone buzzed once more.

"Confirmed. Data verified. Authorities mobilizing. Hold tight. "

It was the message he had been waiting for, yet it brought no comfort. Solomon's network had roots in places Carter couldn't even fathom. Even with authorities involved, there was no telling how far they'd go to silence him.

The barista cleared his untouched coffee, giving him a concerned glance. Carter forced a reassuring nod, though his pulse was anything but calm. He stood, pulling his collar up against the breeze.

The streets of Gibraltar bustled with tourists, their laughter and chatter a jarring contrast to the storm Carter felt brewing around him. Every step down the narrow, winding roads heightened his awareness. He passed storefronts selling souvenirs, cafés crowded with travelers, and small groups of locals chatting in Spanish and English.

But then, just past a shaded alley, Carter saw the unmistakable glint of a polished black sedan creeping along the road. Tinted windows. No plates.

They were watching.

A chill ran through him, but he didn't break stride. Fear wouldn't save him now. He crossed to the opposite side of the street, ducking into a convenience store. Through the glass window, he tracked the sedan as it slowed, then accelerated, disappearing around the corner.

Whoever was in that car wouldn't stay far. Carter grabbed a pack of gum, handed a few coins to the clerk, and slipped back outside. His thoughts shifted to his next move. The local authorities were aware, but that didn't mean Solomon's reach couldn't interfere.

A vibration in his pocket. Another message.

"Rendezvous point. Plaza Mayor. 15 minutes. Stay unseen. "

Carter memorized the instructions and deleted the message. Plaza Mayor wasn't far, but every minute in the open increased his risk. He adjusted his route, zigzagging through the busy streets to avoid being followed.

The plaza came into view — wide, bustling with market stalls and shaded cafés. A perfect location for blending in. He moved through the crowd, heart pounding, scanning faces for any sign of his contact.

A woman in a navy blazer stood near a fountain, speaking into a phone. She never looked directly at him, but Carter recognized her voice as she subtly murmured into the receiver.

"You're clear. Walk past the fountain. The car is waiting. "

Without hesitation, Carter obeyed. He moved past the cascading water, his eyes locked on a silver sedan with tinted windows. But this time, it wasn't an ominous presence — the driver wore an earpiece, a slight nod confirming his intent.

Carter opened the door and slipped inside.

"Mr. Weston," the driver greeted him. "Let's get you somewhere safe."

As the car pulled away, Carter exhaled for what felt like the first time in hours. But even with a moment's respite, one thought remained: It wasn't over yet.

Chapter 49: The Pursuit

The hum of the engine was steady, but Carter couldn't shake the tension in his chest. The driver navigated the narrow streets of Gibraltar with practiced ease, his expression unreadable behind dark sunglasses.

"How much longer?" Carter asked, his voice low.

"Not long," the driver replied without turning his head. "We'll switch vehicles before crossing the border. You'll be safer in Spain. "

Carter nodded, though the reassurance did little to calm him. Solomon's men wouldn't simply give up. The flash drive was out of their reach, but Carter wasn't. And if they suspected that authorities were involved, their desperation could grow.

The sedan twisted through side streets, avoiding the main roads. The driver's calculated movements told Carter everything he needed to know. They weren't just taking precautions — they were being followed.

"How many?" Carter asked, keeping his gaze forward.

"Two vehicles. A black SUV and a silver sedan. Been tailing us since the plaza. "

Carter's jaw tightened. "Options?"

The driver's lips curled into a slight smirk. "We're in Gibraltar. Options are limited, but I have one in mind. Hold on. "

Without further warning, the driver accelerated, weaving through traffic. Horns blared as cars swerved to avoid the sudden maneuver. The black SUV behind them responded immediately, matching the sedan's pace. The silver sedan followed a few lengths behind, maintaining a careful distance.

"Dammit," Carter muttered.

The narrow roads twisted and turned, forcing the pursuers to maintain line-of-sight. But as they approached the harbor, the driver's plan became clear.

"You're not—" Carter began.

"I am," the driver cut him off.

The sedan veered sharply, cutting across lanes and heading straight toward the docks. The road ended abruptly at the water's edge, where large cargo vessels loomed. The driver slammed the brakes, jerking the car to a stop just feet from the water.

"Out," he ordered.

Carter obeyed, adrenaline surging as the driver followed suit. Behind them, the black SUV screeched to a halt. Men in dark suits spilled out, weapons concealed but undoubtedly present.

"Stay close," the driver instructed, leading Carter toward a small motorboat tethered to the dock.

A man in a weathered cap waited, starting the engine the moment they approached.

"Time to go," the boatman grunted.

Carter climbed aboard, and the driver cast one last glance at the approaching men before untying the rope. The engine roared to life, and the small vessel sped away, sending a spray of seawater into the air.

On the dock, the pursuers stood motionless, powerless as the boat disappeared into the open water.

Carter exhaled sharply, his heart pounding. "Where now?"

The driver, now seated across from him, checked his phone before replying.

"We'll cross into Spanish waters. Once we're clear, you'll be transferred to a secure location. Solomon's reach ends here. "

Carter wasn't so sure. Solomon had proven resourceful, and men like him didn't accept defeat easily.

But for now, the chase was over. And with the flash drive in the right hands, Carter had done his part.

Still, the echoes of the pursuit lingered, a stark reminder that even in victory, the fight was far from finished.

Chapter 50: Safe Harbor

The hum of the motorboat softened as they crossed into calmer waters. The salt spray no longer lashed against Carter's face, and the towering cliffs of Gibraltar receded behind them. The driver's stoic expression remained unchanged, though the tension in his shoulders eased.

"We're clear," the boatman announced, cutting the engine to a low idle. The water was a deep, endless blue, with the distant Spanish coastline emerging through the light haze.

Carter shifted uncomfortably, exhaustion settling into his bones. Every muscle ached from the relentless chase, but his mind refused to relax. Even with the flash drive safely backed up and transmitted, Solomon's men wouldn't stop. Carter had witnessed firsthand how far they were willing to go.

"How far to shore?" Carter asked, breaking the silence.

"Less than an hour," the driver replied. "A car will be waiting. From there, you'll be taken to a secure location."

Carter nodded, though the concept of security felt temporary. He gazed out across the open water, the rhythmic sway of the boat lulling him into uneasy reflection.

"What about Solomon?" he finally asked. "He's not the type to let this go."

The driver's expression darkened. "Interpol has the data. That flash drive implicated more than just Solomon. His network is unraveling. It's only a matter of time before they come for him. "

"But that doesn't mean I'm in the clear," Carter muttered.

The driver gave a slight shrug. "No, but it means you're not alone. People are watching out for you now. And Solomon? He'll be too busy saving his own skin. "

Carter wanted to believe it. He wanted to trust that the tide had finally turned. But the shadows of Lagos, the threats that followed him through Casablanca and Gibraltar — they still lingered. The weight of what he'd uncovered, of the corruption and deception, wasn't so easily shaken.

The boatman gestured toward the horizon. "There," he said. "Welcome to Spain."

Carter squinted, catching sight of a small harbor nestled against the coastline. White stucco buildings dotted the hillside, their terracotta roofs glowing in the late afternoon sun. The promise of safety seemed within reach, yet the nagging sense of unfinished business remained.

As the boat pulled alongside the dock, a sleek black SUV was already waiting. A man in a gray suit leaned casually against the vehicle, scanning the water. He straightened as Carter stepped onto the dock, offering a nod of acknowledgment.

"Mr. Weston," the man greeted. "Welcome to Algeciras. I'm with the agency. "

Carter shook his hand firmly. "What now?"

"Now," the agent replied, "we keep you out of sight. There's a secure villa not far from here. You'll have time to rest and regroup. "

"And then?"

The agent's eyes hardened. "And then we'll see how far Solomon's empire crumbles."

Carter exhaled slowly. The journey had taken him across continents, through betrayal and survival. But now, with the evidence in the right hands, the battle shifted.

"Let's go," he said, determination sharpening his tone.

The agent opened the SUV door, and Carter climbed in without another word. The engine roared to life, and as they drove away from the harbor, Carter couldn't help but feel that the storm had only just begun.

Chapter 51: The Villa

The SUV navigated the winding coastal roads, hugging the jagged cliffs as the sun dipped lower on the horizon. The vibrant hues of orange and purple cast a warm glow over the Spanish countryside. Carter gazed out the window, the picturesque landscape in stark contrast to the turmoil he'd left behind.

The agent, still stoic and composed, offered only the occasional glance in the rearview mirror. Carter had grown accustomed to the silence, though the absence of imminent danger felt strangely unsettling. He knew the respite wouldn't last.

After nearly an hour, the SUV pulled off the main road, weaving through olive groves and narrow dirt paths. Nestled at the end of a secluded lane stood a white-washed villa, its terracotta roof and arched doorways exuding Mediterranean charm. Lush bougainvillea cascaded over the stone walls, adding a burst of color to the serene setting.

The agent parked the car and turned to Carter.

"This will be your home for now," he said. "Fully secured. No one gets in or out without us knowing. "

Carter gave a curt nod, the notion of security still ringing hollow.

Inside, the villa was modest yet elegant. A spacious living room with exposed wooden beams opened to a terrace overlooking the sea. The breeze carried the scent of salt and citrus through the open doors. Despite the tranquility, Carter's eyes instinctively scanned for exits and potential threats.

"There's a secure line in the study," the agent continued, leading him down a short hallway. "If you need to contact anyone, use that. The less traceable your movements, the better. "

Carter stepped into the study; the walls lined with dark wooden shelves filled with books that looked untouched. A large desk sat beneath a window; a sleek black phone positioned neatly on its polished surface. He traced his fingers over the desk, the gravity of his isolation settling in.

"I assume I'm not going anywhere?" Carter asked.

The agent's face remained unreadable. "Not yet. But we're working on it. Interpol has enough to begin dismantling Solomon's network. The longer you stay off the radar, the safer you'll be. "

We've discovered his real identity; He's a former intelligence asset turned mercenary middleman for shadow governments and corporations.

He is not after just repatriated funds—he's orchestrating access to Nigeria's entire telecommunications infrastructure to control the flow of information across West Africa.

The "deal" was bait for Carter to serve as a legitimate front.

Carter clenched his jaw. "And Solomon? Any word? "

"He's on the run. His accounts are frozen, assets seized. But men like him don't go down quietly."

Carter nodded slowly. He knew Solomon wasn't just a businessman — he was a survivor. With that kind of money and influence, disappearing was always an option.

The agent's phone buzzed. He checked the screen, his expression hardening.

"Get some rest, Mr. Weston," he said, his tone leaving little room for argument. "We'll update you when we have more."

The door clicked shut, leaving Carter alone in the dim study. The stillness was unnerving. Every muscle in his body ached, the adrenaline that had fueled his escape now replaced with exhaustion. Yet sleep remained elusive.

He wandered onto the terrace, the night air cool against his skin. The darkened coastline stretched endlessly, the faint glimmer of distant ships breaking the horizon. Somewhere out there, Solomon was plotting his next move.

Carter's grip tightened around the railing. He had made it this far. The evidence was out. But the fight wasn't over. Not yet.

Chapter 52: A New Path

The morning sunlight spilled through the villa's large windows, illuminating the rustic wooden beams and terracotta tiles. Carter sat at the kitchen table, nursing a cup of strong black coffee. The events of the past days weighed heavily on him, but for the first time in weeks, there was a semblance of calm.

He had been briefed earlier — Interpol had officially issued warrants for Solomon and several of his associates. The tangled web of corruption had begun to unravel. The digital backup Carter had secured had been instrumental in exposing the illicit operations, and with the right people now in possession of the evidence, the global financial networks Solomon exploited were closing in on him.

Still, the man was a ghost. Carter knew it would take time to bring him in. Powerful people often had escape routes carefully planned. Even so, the once-untouchable facade of Solomon was beginning to crack.

A knock at the door interrupted his thoughts. The agent from the day before entered without ceremony, a secure satellite phone in hand.

"We've got an update," the agent said, placing the phone on the table. "You'll want to hear this."

Carter took a steadying breath and picked up the phone. On the other end was his State Department contact, the voice familiar and calm.

"Carter, I wanted to tell you personally — Solomon's been sighted."

Carter straightened in his chair. "Where?"

"Dubai. He's trying to withdraw funds through one of his remaining shell companies. But we've frozen most of his assets. He's running out of options. "

"Then what's next?"

"Authorities are coordinating. The UAE is cooperative, but he won't go down easy. He's desperate. "

Carter clenched his jaw. He had no doubt Solomon would try to find an escape, perhaps with the help of his remaining allies. But desperation made men reckless. That could be his downfall.

"We'll keep you informed," the contact added. "For now, stay put. You're still a loose end in Solomon's eyes. "

"I understand," Carter replied, though the thought of remaining idle gnawed at him.

After the call ended, the agent lingered. "You've done your part, Carter. Solomon will fall. You don't need to be in the crosshairs anymore. "

Carter nodded, but the words didn't settle easily. He had come too far and risked too much to simply step away. Yet for now, patience was the wisest course.

The sun was just cresting the rooftops when Carter stepped out onto the terrace overlooking the harbor. A dozen sailboats rocked gently in their slips, white hulls gleaming in the morning light. The breeze smelled of salt and memory, and for a moment, he let his mind drift back to his sailing days in the Caribbean. The creak of a boom, the snap of a line, the quiet thrill of watching the horizon unfold.

Then, he heard it—a rustle behind the villa.

Years of instinct kicked in.

He ducked instinctively, shoving the wrought-iron chair aside and drawing his compact sidearm. Two shadowy figures appeared near the garden wall—moving fast, silent, trained.

Solomon's men.

The glass door to the villa exploded inward just as Carter rolled behind the low stone planter. Gunfire barked in the open air, splintering the stucco. He crawled low, heart hammering.

Then—crack-crack!　—Two sharp shots echoed from the rear gate.

A black SUV screeched to a halt in the driveway. Carter's security detail poured out; weapons drawn. One of the attackers went down, the other vanished behind the hedgerow.

"Secure the perimeter!" the lead agent shouted. "Carter, are you hit?"

"No!" Carter barked back, pushing himself to his feet. His pulse roared in his ears, adrenaline surging like a tidal wave.

Within minutes, the threat was neutralized.

One man lay cuffed and bleeding. The other had disappeared, but they had what they needed— proof that Carter was still a target. That Solomon hadn't given up.

Not yet.

The agent approached him, voice tense. "They knew you were here. We got lucky this time."

Carter glanced back at the harbor. The boats bobbed calmly, as if nothing had happened.

"Yeah," he said. "We'll need to be luckier next time."

After everything he had been through, Carter knew he needed an escape plan that didn't involve airports, paper trails, or the ticking of someone else's clock. In the harbor, after a week of careful observation, he found her — a classic 38-foot sloop, moored at the far edge of the harbor, overlooked and underpriced. She was weathered but seaworthy, with good bones and sails that still caught the wind like they remembered adventure.

The owner, a grizzled ex-merchant marine with a head full of stories and a liver full of rum, had grown tired of the sea. Carter made an offer in cash, no questions asked. A handshake sealed it. He registered the boat under a shell company out of Malta — clean, quiet, and untraceable.

He spent a week provisioning and outfitting her for distance sailing, alone in the harbor, his thoughts drifting with the tide.

She didn't have a name when he bought her.

Now she did.

"Second Wind."

The next few days passed with tense updates. Solomon's network crumbled further, his allies abandoning him one by one. With nowhere left to turn, he was forced into hiding. Carter stayed close to the villa, guarded but restless. The sense of finality was near, but the weight of uncertainty remained.

Then, early one morning, the call came.

"It's over, Carter," the voice said simply. "They got him."

Solomon had been apprehended attempting to flee by private yacht. The man who once commanded power through manipulation and fear now sat in the custody of international authorities.

Carter's chest rose with a long breath. Relief. Satisfaction. And yet, a strange emptiness. The chase had defined his days, but now that it was over, the question remained — what next?

He stood on the terrace, gazing out at the endless sea. The wind whispered promises of new beginnings. Perhaps it was time to rebuild, to return to the business he'd once thrived in — only this time with a keener eye for the dangers that lurked beneath the surface.

The choice was his. And for the first time in a long while, Carter Weston felt free.

Chapter 53: Unfinished Business

Carter sat at a seaside café in a quiet Spanish harbor, the salty breeze mixing with the aroma of strong espresso. The sun had barely risen, casting long shadows across the cobblestone streets. Locals moved about with purpose, but Carter's gaze remained fixed on the water, where sailboats bobbed lazily. He couldn't help but think how quickly everything had unraveled.

His instincts had been right all along. The Nigerian deal was a façade — a dangerous ruse that had nearly cost him his life. Yet somehow, he'd made it through. The encrypted drive now in his possession held the evidence, every trace of the scheme carefully cataloged. But what came next?

A sleek black car pulled up across the street, a telltale sign that the conversation he'd been dreading was about to happen. Moments later, two men emerged in tailored suits barely concealing their authority. No introductions were needed. Carter knew their type. Government operatives, clean-cut and composed, with questions they already knew the answers to.

"Mr. Weston," one of them greeted. "Mind if we join you?"

Carter gave a noncommittal shrug. "It's a free country."

They took their seats, the taller of the two removing his sunglasses with a practiced air. "We've been following your movements. You've had quite the adventure. "

"Not one I'd recommend," Carter replied dryly.

The shorter man leaned forward, lowering his voice. "We're interested in what you've uncovered. The drive you're carrying — it could be valuable. "

"And I'm sure you're offering to keep me 'safe' in exchange," Carter replied, his voice laced with sarcasm.

The agent didn't flinch. "We offer opportunities. Resources. A way to ensure something like this never happens again. You've already proven yourself capable. "

Carter shook his head. "I've done my part. The rest is your problem. "

The taller agent slid a small card across the table. "In case you change your mind."

Carter let it sit untouched, his gaze unwavering. "I won't."

They left without another word. The tension dissolved into the morning air, but Carter knew their presence would linger. They'd watch, wait — hoping he'd come around.

But he had no intention of doing so.

Finishing his coffee, Carter stood and made his way toward the docks. His sailboat awaited, the open sea promising a freedom no government agent could offer. Whatever awaited him beyond the horizon, it was his choice alone.

And for now, that was enough.

Chapter 54: Into the Horizon

The gentle creak of the sailboat's mast echoed against the vast emptiness of the open sea. Carter stood at the helm, the steady breeze tugging at the canvas sails as they propelled him forward. The sun had begun its slow descent, painting the sky in streaks of gold and crimson. The coastline of Spain was now a fading silhouette, left behind like the shadows of the past.

The last few days had been a whirlwind — the evasive phone calls, the sudden interest from "representatives" with no clear affiliations. They had come with polished words and thinly veiled questions. Carter didn't need a debriefing to know who they were. Three-letter agencies never announced themselves, but their intentions were clear.

"Your experience could be valuable," one had said.

"We could offer resources, protection, and purpose."

But Carter had already learned that not all offers were worth taking. He'd played their game once — danced through the shadows of corruption and deception. Whatever agenda these people had; it wasn't his to serve. Not yet.

The encrypted drive containing every detail of the Nigerian debacle was stashed below deck, sealed away in a waterproof case. Proof of everything. For now, it was a reminder — a tether to a story he wasn't sure would ever be told.

But as the waves whispered against the hull, Carter let the weight of it all drift away. The Atlantic stretched before him, endless and inviting. No phones. No questions. No past clawing at his heels. Just the horizon, untamed and uncertain.

He adjusted the sails, feeling the wind catch and pull. There was something freeing in the unknown — a new adventure waiting just beyond sight. He wasn't ready to commit to anything. Not to offers, not to alliances. But he was ready to move forward.

For the first time in a long while, Carter smiled.

The sea answered with a rush of salt air. And with that, he sailed on — into the vast blue unknown.

To be continued. ..

Epilogue

After returning from Nigeria, I met with my Congressional Representative to share my experience, hoping it might prompt action and encourage the Nigerian Embassy to issue warnings to the public.

Several weeks after our meeting, full-page ads appeared in multiple business publications, alerting readers to the existence of elaborate international scams. While I felt fortunate to have escaped with little more than a cautionary tale, others were not as lucky.

A highly respected businessman from my area, experienced in North African trade, fell victim to a similar scheme. He and his associates became entangled in a Nigerian oil scam. Among the so-called "Investor Partners, " one man vanished without a trace. To this day, he has never been heard from again and is presumed dead.

The dangers I faced were real, but stories like his serve as a sobering reminder that not everyone escapes the lion's den unscathed.

www.ingramcontent.com/pod-product-compliance
Lightning Source LLC
Chambersburg PA
CBHW062131020426
42335CB00013B/1175